Collins

GCSE Maths

for AQA A

WORKBOOK

GREG BYRD

LYNN BYRD

INTRODUCTION

Welcome to Collins GCSE Maths! This Workbook is designed to help you master the basics of GCSE Mathematics. You will find it contains three main types of page – Help, Practice and Test pages. Here is a quick guide on how to use them.

Help

This page starts you off on a new section with lots of worked examples. It provides you with explanations and hints all the way through. Towards the top of the page, the explanations are quite detailed, but towards the end of the page, you will find there is more work for you to try yourself.

Practice

Once you have worked through the Help page, the Practice page gives you the chance to practice your skills. Remember, if you get really stuck, all the answers are at the back of the book. But do try to work questions out yourself first, as this will help you remember what you have learned better.

Test

The Test pages will let you really prove you understand the Maths, and will help you get ready for the exams. Note that each Test contains questions from more than one section. This will help keep the key ideas you have learned fresh in your mind.

At the top right of each page you will notice three circles. These are for you to mark in how well you feel you have understood everything on that page. For example…

I have started this section but I don't completely understand it yet.

I am getting better, but I have not yet been able to complete the exercises correctly.

I completely understand this section, and have completed all the exercises correctly.

We hope you find this Workbook useful. Good luck with your studies!

Your name……………………………

Class …………………………………

CONTENTS

Chapter 1

Addition   6
Subtraction   8
Multiplication   10
Division   12
BODMAS (BIDMAS)   14
Place value and rounding   16

Test 1   18

Chapter 2

Fractions – shading and adding   20
Fractions – equivalent and cancelling   22
Fractions – top heavy and mixed numbers   24
Fractions – of an amount

Test 2   28

Chapter 3   Negative numbers   30

Chapter 4   Multiples and Factors   32
Square, square root and powers   34

Chapter 5   Shapes – area   36

Test 3   38
Shapes – perimeter   40

Chapter 6   Statistics – frequency tables and charts   42

Chapter 7   Algebra – writing expressions   46

Test 4   48
Algebra – using formulae and sequences   50

Chapter 8   Decimal rounding   52

Chapter 9   Ratio   54

Chapter 10   Symmetry   56

Chapter 11	Averages – mean, median, mode, range	58
Test 5		60
Chapter 12	Percentages, decimals and fractions	62
	Percentage of a quantity	64
Chapter 13	Algebra – solving equations	66
Chapter 14	Conversion graphs	68
	Plotting points and naming shapes	70
Test 6		72
Chapter 15	Angles	74
Chapter 16	Circles	76
Chapter 17	Scale drawing and nets	78
Test 7		80
Chapter 18	Probability	82
Chapter 19	Transformations	84
Chapter 21	Units	86
Test 8		88
Chapter 22	Pie charts	90
Chapter 24	Volume of 3-D shapes	92
Test 9		94
Answers to Help questions		96
Answers to Practice questions		102
Answers to Test questions		108

You need to know:

- How to add integers (whole numbers) ● How to add decimal numbers

EXAMPLE 1

Find the sum of 8 and 5.

8 + 5 = 13, the 3 is worth 3 units, so keep it in the units column

```
H T U
    8
    5 +
  1 3
```

> **Remember:**
> 'Find the sum of' means 'add together'.

EXAMPLE 2

Add together 168 and 315.

Always start with the units. 8 + 5 = 13, so put the 3 in the units column and carry the 1 into the tens column. Then add the tens, 6 + 1 + 1 = 8, then add the hundreds, 1 + 3 = 4

```
H T U
1 6 8
3 1 5 +
4 8 3
  1
```

> **Remember:**
> The column headings are **U**nits, **T**ens, **H**undreds etc.

Question 1

Work out these additions.

a
```
  3 4 8
  4 6 8 +
      6
      1
```

Start with 8 + 8 = 16
Put the 6 in the units column and carry the 1 to the tens column
Then add 4 + 6 + 1 = ... Remember to carry if the answer is more than 10

b
```
  1 3 4 8
  5 4 6 8 +
        6
        1
```

> Complete the workings for these two additions.

Question 2

Fill in the missing digits to complete this addition sum.

```
□ 1 7
2 □ 5 +
6 2 □
```

Step 1: Units first. 7 + 5 = 12, put the 2 in the units box, carry the 1.
Step 2: Tens next.
You have 1 + ? + 1 = 2. What goes in the box?
Step 3: Finally the hundreds ? + 2 = 6

> Follow the steps and put the numbers in the empty boxes.

Question 3

Fill in the missing digits to complete this addition sum.

```
  4 4 7 9
□ □ □ □ □ +
  6 0 8 8
```

> **Hint:** 9 + ? = 8, nothing works, but 9 + ? = 18 can be done.

Question 4

Evaluate the following:

a 26.7 + 18.4

Step 1: Set it out properly and keep the decimal points in line
Step 2: Add like normal

```
T U . Tth
2 6 . 7
1 8 . 4 +
    . 1
    1
```

> Evaluate just means work out. **T**th is the tenths column.

b 41.6 + 2.24

This is a tricky one, but follow the steps above, and fill any empty spaces with zeros to help you

```
4 1 . 6
  2 . 2 4 +
    . 4
```

> Complete the workings for these two decimal additions.

1 Write down the answers to each of the following addition sums.

a
```
    5
    7 +
  ___
```

b
```
   7 3
   5 2 +
  ____
```

c
```
  1 7 3
  2 5 7 +
  _____
```

d
```
  1 7 5 0
    4 3 8 +
  _____
```

e 634 + 936

```
  _____ +
  _____
```

Set it out properly first

2 Fill in the missing digits to complete these addition sums.

a
```
    8
   □ +
  □ 4
```

b
```
   □ 4
   8 □ +
   1 1 1
```

c
```
  1 2 8 4
  □ □ □ +
  1 7 2 0
```

3 Evaluate the following decimal addition sums:

a
```
  2 7 . 8
    8 . 3 +
  _____.___
```

b
```
  1 7 . 8
    4 . 2 2 +
  _____.____
```

c
```
        2 . 1
  2 1 7 . 4 2 2 +
  _____.____
```

Set **d** and **e** out properly before adding.

d 16.4 + 9.9

```
  _____.____ +
  _____.____
```

e 8.4 + 21.66

```
  _____.____ +
  _____.____
```

4 Darren has £135 in the bank.
He pays in another £47.
How much does he now have in the bank?

```
  _____ +
  _____
```

5 Sam buys a skirt costing £13.99 and a top costing £8.75.
What is the total cost of these items?

```
  _____.____ +
  _____.____
```

6 The attendance at a cinema on Saturday is:
376 people in the afternoon and
545 people in the evening.
What is the total number of people at the cinema on Saturday?

```
  _____ +
  _____
```

You need to know:

- How to take away integers (whole numbers) • How to take away decimal numbers

EXAMPLE 1

Take away 28 from 49.

$$\begin{array}{cc} T & U \\ 4 & 9 \\ 2 & 8 - \\ \hline 2 & 1 \end{array}$$

Step 1: Units first. $9 - 8 = 1$
Step 2: Tens next. $4 - 2 = 2$

Always set up the subtraction with the smaller number underneath the larger.

EXAMPLE 2

Subtract 46 from 83.

$$\begin{array}{cc} {}^7\!\cancel{8} & {}^1 3 \\ 4 & 6 - \\ \hline \end{array}$$

Step 1: Units first.
$3 - 6$ cannot be done,
so borrow from the 8

Example 2 shows the 'borrowing' method.

$$\begin{array}{cc} {}^7\!\cancel{8} & {}^1 3 \\ 4 & 6 - \\ \hline 3 & 7 \end{array}$$

Step 2: Units can now be done. $13 - 6 = 7$
Step 3: Tens next. $7 - 4 = 3$

Question 1

Work out these subtractions.

a
$$\begin{array}{ccc} 3 & 7 & 0 \\ 1 & 3 & 7 - \\ \hline \end{array}$$

Step 1: Units first. $0 - 7$ cannot be done, so borrow from the 7
Step 2: Units can now be done. $10 - 7 = 3$
Step 3: Continue one column at a time

$$\begin{array}{ccc} 3 & {}^6\!\cancel{7} & {}^1 0 \\ 1 & 3 & 7 - \\ \hline & & 3 \end{array}$$

Complete the workings in question 1. Be careful in **b**, you will need to borrow twice.

b
$$\begin{array}{cccc} 5 & 3 & 7 & 5 \\ 2 & 5 & 2 & 6 - \\ \hline \end{array}$$

Step 1: Units first. $5 - 6$ can't be done, borrow from the 7
Step 2: Units can now be done. $15 - 6 = 9$
Step 3: Continue one column at a time

$$\begin{array}{cccc} 5 & 3 & {}^6\!\cancel{7} & {}^1 5 \\ 2 & 5 & 2 & 6 - \\ \hline & & & 9 \end{array}$$

Question 2

Fill in the missing digits to complete the subtractions.

a
$$\begin{array}{ccc} 8 & 5 \\ 4 & \square - \\ \hline \square & 2 \end{array}$$

Step 1: $5 - ? = 2$
Step 2: $8 - 4 = ?$

b
$$\begin{array}{cccc} 8 & {}^0\!\cancel{1} & {}^1 1 & 9 \\ \square & \square & \square & \square - \\ \hline 5 & 1 & 5 & 9 \end{array}$$

Step 1: $9 - ? = 9$

Step 2: Be careful!
$1 - ? = 5$ can't be done,
so borrow from the 1,
giving $11 - ? = 5$

Complete the workings and fill in the boxes in both parts of this question.

Question 3

Work out each of these: **a** $8.1 - 2.7$ **b** $18.25 - 4.5$

a
$$\begin{array}{ccc} 8 & . & 1 \\ 2 & . & 7 - \\ \hline & . & \end{array}$$

Step 1: $1 - 7$ can't be done, borrow from the 8
Step 2: The subtraction can now be done

b
$$\begin{array}{ccccc} 1 & 8 & . & 2 & 5 \\ 0 & 4 & . & 5 & 0 - \\ \hline & & . & & 5 \end{array}$$

Step 1: Fill in any blank spaces with zeros
Step 2: $5 - 0 = 5$
Step 3: $2 - 5$ can't be done, so borrow from the 8
Step 4: Complete the subtraction

Complete these decimal subtractions.

Remember: Line up the numbers so the decimal points are underneath each other.

1 Work out the following subtractions.

a 9 8
   4 6 −
   ———

b 9 6
   4 8 −
   ———

c 9 0
   4 6 −
   ———

d 5 4 4 6
   2 5 1 8 −
   —————

e 140 − 82
   ——————— −

Set it out properly first

2 Fill in the missing digits to complete these subtractions.

a 2 8
   1 □ −
   □ 6

b 3 7 □
   1 □ 5 −
   □ 2 8

c 5 2 5 2
   □ □ □ □ −
   2 7 2 7

3 Evaluate the following decimal subtractions:

a 8 . 4
   5 . 7 −
   ———

b 9 .
   4 . 2 −
   ———

c 4 . 2 5
   2 . 5   −
   ———

Set **d** and **e** out properly before subtracting.

d 32 − 9.6

e 6.54 − 1.81

4 Jo has £278 in the bank.
She takes out £45.
How much does she have left in the bank?

5 Paul has a piece of wood 125cm long.
He cuts a 48 cm piece from one end.
How long is the piece that is left?

6 Dave gets a credit card bill for £359.65.
He pays £175.
How much does he still owe?

You need to know:

- Your times tables from 1 x 1 to 10 x 10
- How to do long multiplication
- How to multiply decimal numbers

EXAMPLE 1

Multiply 17 by 5.

Step 1: $7 \times 5 = 35$, put the 5 in the units column and carry the 3 to the tens column

```
  1 7
    5 ×
    5
  3
```

Step 2: $1 \times 5 = 5$, then add the 3 to give $5 + 3 = 8$

```
  1 7
    5 ×
  8 5
  3
```

Always set up the multiplication with the smaller number underneath the larger.

EXAMPLE 2

Calculate 321 times 38.

Step 1: Multiply the 321 by 8. $1 \times 8 = 8$, $2 \times 8 = 16$, put the 6 down and carry the 1, $3 \times 8 = 24$ plus the $1 = 25$

```
    3 2 1
      3 8 ×
    2 5 6 8
        1
```

Step 2: Multiply the 321 by 30, so put a zero down first, then do 321×3:
$1 \times 3 = 3$
$2 \times 3 = 6$
$3 \times 3 = 9$

```
      3 2 1
        3 8 ×
    2 5 6 8
          1

    9 6 3 0
```

Example 2 is more complicated - two extra lines of working are needed.

Remember: the 3 is worth 30, so put a 0 down first.

Step 3: Final step is to add the two lines of working together starting with the units on the right:
$8 + 0 = 8$
$6 + 3 = 9$
$5 + 6 = 11$ put down the 1 and carry the other 1
$9 + 2 + 1 = 12$

```
      3 2 1
        3 8 ×
    2 5 6 8
          1
    9 6 3 0
  1 2 1 9 8
          1
```

Question 1

Calculate the following: **a** 12×8 **b** 29×42

a
```
  1 2
    8 ×
  ___
```

Step 1: $2 \times 8 = 16$, put the 6 in the units column and carry the 1 to the tens column

Step 2: $1 \times 8 = ?$, then add the 1 you carried

b
```
    2 9
    4 2 ×
      8
      1

    6 0
    3

      8
```

Step 1: 29×2

Step 2: 29×40, so start with a 0

Step 3: Add together the 2 lines of working to get your final answer

Follow the steps to complete the multiplication.

Complete the workings for this question.

Question 2

What is 7×4.6?

Step 1: Ignore the decimal point and work out 46×7

```
  4 6
    7 ×
    2
  4
```

Step 2: When multiplying decimals, count how many numbers are after the decimal point in the question – in this case one, and so one number must be after the point in the answer.

$4.6 \times 7 =$ _____

Finish the multiplication.

Write your final answer here.

1 Work out the following:

a   1 4
  $\underline{\quad 7} \times$

b   3 5
  $\underline{\quad 7} \times$

c   2 4 1
  $\underline{\qquad 7} \times$

Set **d** and **e** out properly before multiplying.

d 164×5

  $\underline{\qquad\qquad} \times$

e 206×4

  $\underline{\qquad\qquad} \times$

2 Calculate the following:

a   1 4
  $\underline{\quad 2\ 7} \times$

  $\underline{\qquad} +$

b   3 5
  $\underline{\quad 3\ 7} \times$

  $\underline{\qquad} +$

c   4 1
  $\underline{\quad 2\ 7} \times$

  $\underline{\qquad} +$

3 Evaluate the following:

a   2 3 4
  $\underline{\qquad 1\ 6} \times$

  $\underline{\qquad\quad} +$

b   2 5 7
  $\underline{\qquad 3\ 5} \times$

  $\underline{\qquad\quad} +$

c   6 0 6
  $\underline{\qquad 2\ 6} \times$

  $\underline{\qquad\quad} +$

4 Multiply the following:

a   2 3 . 4
  $\underline{\qquad 6} \times$

b   0 . 4 4
  $\underline{\qquad 7} \times$

c   9 . 0 5
  $\underline{\qquad 5} \times$

5 A school orders 12 coaches for a school trip.
Each coach holds 52 people.
How many people can go on the trip?

  $\underline{\qquad\qquad} \times$

  $\underline{\qquad\qquad} +$

  $\underline{\qquad\qquad}$

You need to know:

- How to divide integers (whole numbers) and decimal numbers
- Your times-tables from 1×1 to 10×10

EXAMPLE 1

What is $42 \div 6$?

You may do this in your head, but get used to setting all division questions like this:

$$6 \overline{\smash{)}\,4\,2} \qquad 6 \overline{\smash{)}\,4^4\,2} \qquad 6 \overline{\smash{)}\,4^4\,2}$$

(answer 0)   (answer 0)   (answer 0 7)

Step 1: $4 \div 6$, or how many 6s go into 4? None, so put down the 0 and carry the 4

Step 2: $42 \div 6$, or how many 6s go into 42? 7 exactly with no remainder to carry

> Don't forget to carry the remainder on when there is one.

EXAMPLE 2

What is $504 \div 21$?

$$21 \overline{\smash{)}\,5^5\,0\,4} \qquad 21 \overline{\smash{)}\,5^5\,0^8\,4} \qquad 21 \overline{\smash{)}\,5^5\,0^8\,4}$$

(answer 0)   (answer 0 2)   (answer 0 2 4)

Step 1: $5 \div 21 = ?$ none, can't do it, so carry the 5 on

Step 2: $50 \div 21 = 2$ (look at the 21 times table) There is a remainder of 8 to carry on $(50 - 42 = 8)$

Step 3: $84 \div 21 = 4$ exactly, no remainder to carry on

> Any good at your 21 times table? Most people aren't, so work it out before you start.
> $1 \times 21 = 21$
> $2 \times 21 = 42$
> $3 \times 21 = 63$
> $4 \times 21 = 84$
> $5 \times 21 = 105$
> $6 \times 21 = 126$
> $7 \times 21 = 147$
> $8 \times 21 = 168$
> $9 \times 21 = 189$

Question 1

What is $642 \div 6$?

Re-write as:

$$6 \overline{\smash{)}\,6\,4\,2} \qquad 6 \overline{\smash{)}\,6\,4^4\,2} \qquad 6 \overline{\smash{)}\,6\,4^4\,2}$$

(answer 1)   (answer 1 0)   (answer 1 0)

Step 1: $6 \div 6 = 1$ with no remainder to carry on

Step 2: $4 \div 6 = 0$, can't do it, so carry the 4 on

Step 3: $42 \div 6 = ?$

> Complete **Step 3** in this question.

Question 2

What is $67.8 \div 3$?

Re-write as:

$$3 \overline{\smash{)}\,6\,7\,.\,8}$$

(answer 2 .)

Step 1: Put the decimal point in the answer directly above the one in the question. Then start with $6 \div 3 = 2$ with no remainder

> Complete the remaining steps in this question.

Question 3

A lottery win of £53,172 is to be shared between 7 people. How much does each one get?

$$7 \overline{\smash{)}\,5^5\,3^4\,1\,7\,2}$$

(answer 0 7)

> Complete this division. Don't forget to carry the remainder when there is one.

1 Work out the following divisions:

a $2 \overline{)4\ 6}$ b $2 \overline{)3\ 8}$ c $2 \overline{)5\ 3\ 2}$ d $2 \overline{)7\ 1\ 6}$

2 Calculate the following:

a $6 \overline{)7\ 3\ 8}$ b $5 \overline{)6\ 0\ 5}$ c $7 \overline{)1\ 5\ 5\ 4}$ d $4 \overline{)2\ 5\ 6\ 0}$

3 Evaluate:

a $3 \overline{)9\ 3\ .\ 6}$ b $3 \overline{)1\ 8\ .\ 6}$ c $3 \overline{)5\ 2\ .\ 2}$

4 Work out these:

a $15 \overline{)1\ 8\ .\ 4\ 5}$ b $15 \overline{)5\ .\ 1\ 7\ 5}$

5 Calculate each of the following (set them out properly first).

a $64.8 \div 4$ _____   b $2.415 \div 7$ _____

6 Four friends win a total of £2184. They share it equally
between them. How much do they each get? _____

7 Carol goes on a walking holiday. She plans to walk
105 miles in 7 days. How far is this each day? _____

8 Paul buys a new sofa for £672. He pays for the
sofa over 12 months. He pays the same amount each
month. How much does he pay each month? _____

You need to know:

● In what order you calculate things when more than one maths sign ($+ - \times \div$) is involved

1st	B	= Brackets ( )
2nd	O or I	= Order or Indices ^{2} $^3\sqrt{}$
3rd	DM	= Division and Multiplication $\div \times$
4th	AS	= Addition and Subtraction $+ -$

2×3 is done first because M comes before A.

EXAMPLE 1

$2 \times 3 + 4 = \mathbf{6} + 4 = 10$

EXAMPLE 2

$2 + 3 \times 4 = 2 + \mathbf{12} = 14$

3×4 is done first because M comes before A.

Notice in these first two examples they both have 2,3,4, + and x, but different answers.

Question 1

$5 \times 10 - 1 = \underline{} - 1 = \underline{}$

Question 2

$10 - 10 \div 5 = \underline{} - \underline{} = 8$

Question 3

$5 + 6 - 7 = \underline{}$

Fill in the blank spaces for questions 1 to 3.

+ and − are both in 4th place, so they can be done in whatever order you find easiest; probably $5 + 6 = 11$, $11 - 7 = ?$

Question 4

$3 \times (3 + 6) = 3 \times 9 = \underline{}$

Question 5

$2 \times (6 - 2) = 2 \text{ x } \underline{} = \underline{}$

Question 6

$(3 \times 2) + 10 = \underline{} + \underline{} = 16$

Question 7

$(5 + 15) \div 2 = \underline{} \div 2 = \underline{}$

Fill in the blank spaces for questions 4 to 7.

Remember: Always do the brackets first.

Question 8

Draw lines connecting the question on the left, to the working in the middle, to the answer on the right.

$4 + 3 \times 3$	=	$12 - 2$	=	18
$5 + (8 \div 4)$	=	9×2	=	10
$12 - 6 \div 3$	=	$13 - 4$	=	13
$(4 + 5) \times 2$	=	$4 + 9$	=	7
$8 + 5 - 4$	=	$5 + 2$	=	9

Draw lines to join the question, working and answer together. Some have been started for you. **Hint:** use different colours.

1 Work out each of these:

a $3 \times 2 + 5 = $ _____

b $4 \times 4 + 4 = $ _____

c $4 \times 4 \div 2 = $ _____

d $4 \times 4 - 4 = $ _____

e $5 + 3 \times 2 = $ _____

f $4 + 4 \times 4 = $ _____

g $4 \div 2 \times 4 = $ _____

h $4 - 4 + 4 = $ _____

i $5 \times 6 + 4 \times 2 = $ _____

2 Evaluate the following:

a $2 \times (3 + 3) = $ _____

b $10 \div (3 + 2) = $ _____

c $(3 + 7) \div 2 = $ _____

d $(3 + 7) \times 5 = $ _____

e $5 \times (2 + 3) = $ _____

f $6 \times (3 - 2) = $ _____

g $(5 + 2) \times 3 = $ _____

h $(6 + 3) \times 2 = $ _____

i $(5 + 7) \div 4 = $ _____

3 Draw lines connecting the question on the left with the correct answer on the right.

a $2 \times 2 + 6$

b $2 + 6 \div 3$

c $5 - 1 \times 4$

d $(3 + 5) \div 4$

e $4 \times (5 - 2)$

f $20 \div (7 - 3)$

i 1

ii 12

iii 10

iv 5

v 2

vi 4

4 Are the following statements True (**T**) or False (**F**)?

a $12 + 6 \div 3 = 6$ _____

b $14 - 4 \times 2 = 20$ _____

c $16 \div 2 + 2 = 10$ _____

d $8 - 2 \times 2 = 4$ _____

5 In each question, put in brackets to make the answer correct.

a $4 \times 2 + 1 = 12$

b $2 \times 8 - 5 = 6$

c $12 \div 3 + 3 = 7$

d $4 + 2 \times 4 = 24$

e $12 - 3 \times 3 = 3$

f $3 + 3 \times 4 = 24$

6 In each question put in $+$, $-$, $\times$, $\div$, or brackets to make the answer correct.

a 2   3   4 $= 20$

b 2   3   4 $= 2$

c 2   3   4 $= 1$

d 2   3   4 $= 14$

You need to know:
● How to work out the value of any digit in a number ● How to round off a number to the nearest 10, 100 and 100

Place value

Remember HTU? Hundreds, Tens, and Units – but you need to know more:

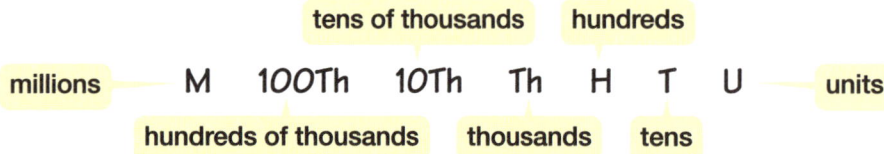

tens of thousands hundreds

millions — M 100Th 10Th Th H T U — units

hundreds of thousands thousands tens

EXAMPLE 1

Give the value of the underlined digit.

a 3<u>7</u>1   Put H T U over the top: H T U / 3 <u>7</u> 1   **Answer** = 7 tens **or** 70

b <u>1</u>7,011   Put 10Th Th HTU over the top: 10th th H T U / <u>1</u> 7, 0 1 1

Answer = 1 tens of thousands = ten thousand **or** 10,000

Question 1

Give the value of the underlined digit.

a 4<u>2</u>35   Th H T U / 4 <u>2</u> 3 5   Answer = _____

b 164<u>0</u>   Th H T U / 1 6 4 <u>0</u>   Answer = _____

c <u>8</u>97,171   100Th 10Th Th H T U / <u>8</u> 9 7, 1 7 1   Answer = _____

Rounding

EXAMPLE 2

Round 184 to the nearest 10.

When going up in tens, 184 is between 180 and 190.
It is nearer to 180 than 190, so

Answer = 180

EXAMPLE 3

Round 82,150 to the nearest 100.

When going up in hundreds 82,150 is between 82,100 and 82,200.
But which is nearer? Neither; 82,150 is exactly half way between 82,100 and 82,200,
and we always round up

Answer = 82,200

Question 2

Round 25 to the nearest 10   Answer = _____

Question 3

Round 2070 to the nearest 100   Answer = _____

Remember:
4 thousands can be written as 4 thousand **or** 4000.

Remember:
4 tens of thousands can be written as 40 thousand **or** 40,000.

Remember:
4 hundreds of thousands can be written as 4 hundred thousand **or** 400,000.

Fill in the answers to question 1.

Fill in the answers to questions 2 and 3.

Hint: 25 is exactly half way between 20 and 30.

Hint: Between 2000 and 2100.

1 Fill in the gaps in this place value diagram.

Millions	Hundreds of Thousands		Thousands	Hundreds		Units

2 Write down the value of the underlined digit in each of these numbers.

Hint: Use the place value diagram to help

a 471 03<u>6</u> _____

b 4<u>7</u>1 036 _____

c 471 <u>0</u>36 _____

d 814 3<u>9</u>5 _____

e <u>8</u>14 395 _____

f 81<u>4</u> 395 _____

3 Write these numbers in order putting the smallest first.

a 800, 567, 129, 378, 99, 210, 201 _____

b 929, 292, 2009, 333, 303, 112, 12 _____

4 Round off each of these numbers to the given amount.

a 75 to the nearest 10 _____

b 75 to the nearest 100 _____

c 3075 to the nearest 100 _____

d 3075 to the nearest 1000 _____

e 27 450 to the nearest 1000 _____

f 27 450 to the nearest 100 _____

g 1750 to the nearest 100 _____

h 999 to the nearest 10 _____

Careful with **h**; it's a tricky one!

5 Which of these statements are true (**T**) and which are false (**F**)?

Arsenal V Chelsea

Attendance: 32 459

a The attendance at Arsenal v Chelsea was 32 000 to the nearest 1000 _____

b The attendance at Arsenal v Chelsea was 32 400 to the nearest 100 _____

c The attendance at Arsenal v Chelsea was 32 500 to the nearest 100 _____

d The attendance at Arsenal v Chelsea was 32 450 to the nearest 10 _____

1 Write down the answer to each of the following questions.

a
```
  7 3 0
  4 4 4  +
  ─────
```

b
```
  3 7 . 4
    9 . 8 2  +
  ─────────
```

c Add £17.99 and £18.75   £
```
£              +
─────────
```

d
```
  2 7 . 7 4
  3 □ . 1 □  +
  □ 4 . □ 6
```

e
```
  7 3 0
  4 4 4  −
  ─────
```

f
```
  3 7 . 4
    9 . 8 2  −
  ─────────
```

g Subtract £105 from £322.50
```
£
£              −
─────────
```

h
```
  6 2
    6  ×
  ───
```

i
```
  3 6 2
      6  ×
  ─────
```

j
```
  3 6 2
    4 6  ×
  ─────
```

k
```
  3 . 6 2
        4  ×
  ───────
```

l Find 8 lots of £5.75   £
```
£              ×
─────────
```

m 2 ⟌ 1 1 4 6

n 6 ⟌ 1 4 5 . 8

o Divide £6132 by 12

p $3 \times 2 + 5 =$ _____

q $3 + 2 \times 5 =$ _____

r $3 \times 6 + 4 \div 2 =$ _____

s $(8 + 2) \div 2 =$ _____

t $8 + 2 \div 2 =$ _____

u $8 \div (2 + 2) =$ _____

2 Give the value of the underlined digit in the following numbers.

a 413,0<u>2</u>9 _____

b 4<u>1</u>3,029 _____

18

3 Round these numbers to the given amount.

   a 49,495 to the nearest 10 _____

   b 49,495 to the nearest 100 _____

   c 49,495 to the nearest 1000 _____

4 Complete this shopping bill:

   4 kg of apples at £0.75 per kilo   _____

   3 kg of bananas at £0.80 per kilo   _____

   7 cans of custard at 89p per can   _____

                                  Total   _____

5 Chad buys 8 pens. Each pen costs 85p.
How much change does he get when he pays with a £10 note?

_____

_____

_____

_____

6 An egg weighs 50 g, and an egg box weighs 15 g.
Find the total weight of a box with 6 eggs in it.

_____

_____

_____

_____

You need to know:
- How to shade a fraction of a shape and recognise what fraction has been shaded
- How to add and subtract fractions with the same denominator

EXAMPLE 1

What fraction of these shapes are shaded?

a   Answer = $\frac{3}{8}$ 3 parts are shaded / 8 equal parts

b   Answer = $\frac{11}{12}$ 11 parts are shaded / 12 equal parts

Hint: When deciding what fraction of a shape is shaded, ask yourself these questions: How many equal parts are there? How many parts are shaded?

EXAMPLE 2

Shade in $\frac{5}{6}$ of this shape: Answer =   5 parts shaded out of the 6

Remember: The shapes must be divided into equal size parts.

Question 1

a What fraction of this shape is shaded?

b What fraction of this shape is unshaded?

a Answer = $\frac{\square}{\square}$ parts shaded / number of equal parts

b Answer = $\frac{\square}{\square}$ parts unshaded

Complete the fractions in question 1.

Question 2

Shade $\frac{2}{3}$ of this shape: Answer =

Complete question 2 **Remember:** $\frac{2}{3}$ — shade this many / total number of equal parts

EXAMPLE 3

Calculate each of the following:

a $\frac{3}{7} + \frac{3}{7}$ Answer = $\frac{3}{7} + \frac{3}{7} = \frac{6}{7}$ (3 + 3)

Do not add the 7s
3 sevenths + 3 sevenths = 6 sevenths
not 6 fourteenths

b $\frac{9}{11} - \frac{4}{11}$ Answer = $\frac{9}{11} - \frac{4}{11} = \frac{5}{11}$

Remember: The denominator is the number at the bottom of the fraction (the number of equal parts).

Question 3

Calculate each of the following:

a $\frac{7}{8} - \frac{2}{8} = \frac{\square}{8}$ b $\frac{9}{10} - \frac{3}{10} = \frac{6}{\square}$

c $\frac{4}{20} + \frac{7}{20} = \frac{\square}{\square}$ d $\frac{2}{9} + \frac{\square}{9} = \frac{5}{9}$

Fill in the boxes to complete question 3.

1 What fraction of each of these shapes is shaded?

a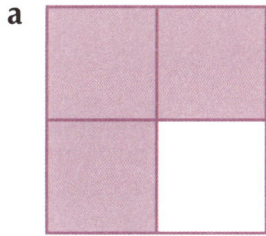

b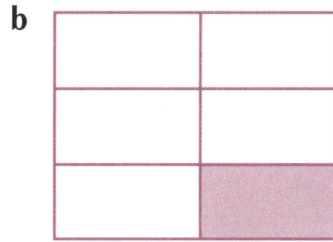

c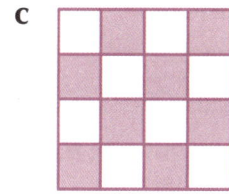

_____   _____   _____

2 Shade in the fraction indicated underneath each shape.

a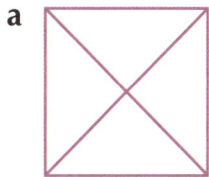

$\dfrac{3}{4}$

b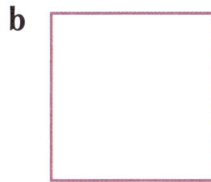

$\dfrac{1}{4}$

c

$\dfrac{2}{3}$

d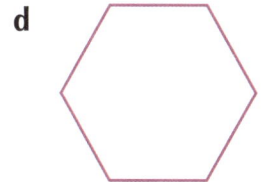

$\dfrac{1}{6}$

3 Calculate each of the following:

a $\dfrac{3}{7} + \dfrac{2}{7} =$ _____

b $\dfrac{2}{5} + \dfrac{2}{5} =$ _____

c $\dfrac{7}{8} - \dfrac{5}{8} =$ _____

d $\dfrac{7}{20} - \dfrac{3}{20} =$ _____

4 Draw lines linking the questions on the left to the answers on the right.

a $\dfrac{3}{8} + \dfrac{2}{8} =$

b $\dfrac{5}{6} - \dfrac{3}{6} =$

c $\dfrac{15}{16} - \dfrac{10}{16} =$

d $\dfrac{1}{3} + \dfrac{1}{3} =$

i $\dfrac{5}{16}$

ii $\dfrac{2}{3}$

iii $\dfrac{5}{8}$

iv $\dfrac{2}{6}$

5 a Draw a diagram to show: $\dfrac{2}{4}$

b Show on your diagram that: $\dfrac{2}{4} = \dfrac{1}{2}$

Hint: Start by drawing a square or rectangle and dividing it up into 4 equal parts

c Use the information from 5 **a** and **b** to write down the answers to:

i $\dfrac{1}{2} + \dfrac{1}{4} =$ _____

ii $\dfrac{1}{2} - \dfrac{1}{4} =$ _____

21

You need to know:

- How to create equivalent fractions
- How to cancel down fractions

EXAMPLE 1

Write down the equivalent fractions shown by the following diagrams.

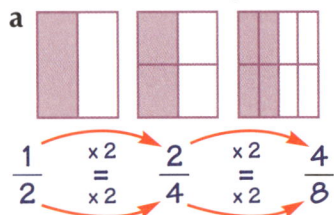

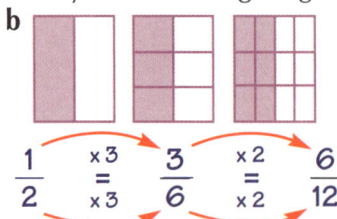

a

$$\frac{1}{2} \xrightarrow[\times 2]{\times 2} \frac{2}{4} \xrightarrow[\times 2]{\times 2} \frac{4}{8}$$

b

$$\frac{1}{2} \xrightarrow[\times 3]{\times 3} \frac{3}{6} \xrightarrow[\times 2]{\times 2} \frac{6}{12}$$

EXAMPLE 2

Cancel down $\frac{10}{20}$ to its lowest terms.

> To cancel down a fraction we need to divide the top and bottom of the fraction by the same number. To cancel down $\frac{10}{20}$ we can either do:

$$\frac{10}{20} \xrightarrow[\div 10]{\div 10} \frac{1}{2} \quad \text{or} \quad \frac{10}{20} \xrightarrow[\div 2]{\div 2} \frac{5}{10} \xrightarrow[\div 5]{\div 5} \frac{1}{2} \qquad \textbf{Answer} = \frac{1}{2}$$

Question 1

Draw a line between each fraction on the top to its equivalent fraction on the bottom.

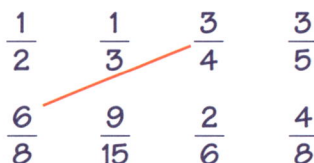

$$\frac{1}{2} \qquad \frac{1}{3} \qquad \frac{3}{4} \qquad \frac{3}{5}$$

$$\frac{6}{8} \qquad \frac{9}{15} \qquad \frac{2}{6} \qquad \frac{4}{8}$$

Question 2

Complete this statement to give two equivalent fractions.

$$\frac{2}{3} \xrightarrow[\times 2]{\times 2} \frac{\square}{6} \xrightarrow[\times ?]{\times ?} \frac{20}{\square}$$

Question 3

Cancel down this fraction:

$$\frac{40}{100} \xrightarrow[\div 10]{\div 10} \frac{4}{10} \xrightarrow[\div ?]{\div ?} \frac{\square}{\square}$$

Question 4

Which fraction is the biggest; $\frac{1}{2}$, $\frac{5}{6}$, $\frac{2}{3}$?

$$\frac{1}{2} = \frac{\square}{6} \qquad \frac{5}{6} = \frac{5}{6} \qquad \frac{2}{3} = \frac{\square}{6} \qquad \text{Answer: biggest} = \frac{\square}{\square}$$

Remember: Equivalent fractions are equal in size.

Hint: To find an equivalent fraction, simply multiply the top and bottom of the fraction by the same number.

Remember: When a fraction is in its lowest terms it cannot be cancelled down any more.

Complete question 1. One pair of equivalent fractions has already been done for you.

Fill in the boxes to complete the equivalent fractions.

Remember: whatever you times the top by, you must times the bottom by.

Fill in the boxes to cancel down this fraction to its lowest terms.

Hint: What can you divide both 4 and 10 by?

Compare these fractions by changing them all into sixths.

1 Complete each of these statements:

a $\dfrac{1}{2} = \dfrac{2}{\square} = \dfrac{\square}{6} = \dfrac{4}{\square} = \dfrac{\square}{10} = \dfrac{\square}{20}$

b $\dfrac{3}{5} = \dfrac{6}{\square} = \dfrac{9}{\square} = \dfrac{\square}{20} = \dfrac{\square}{25} = \dfrac{30}{\square}$

> Be careful with the last ones – draw a fraction diagram if it helps.

2 Join the pairs of equivalent fractions with a line.

$\dfrac{1}{2}$ $\dfrac{1}{3}$ $\dfrac{1}{4}$

$\dfrac{6}{20}$ $\dfrac{5}{20}$ $\dfrac{5}{10}$ $\dfrac{10}{30}$

$\dfrac{2}{5}$ $\dfrac{3}{10}$ $\dfrac{4}{10}$

> Every fraction should be joined to one other fraction.

3 Cancel down each of the following fractions.

a $\dfrac{6}{20} =$ _____

b $\dfrac{20}{30} =$ _____

c $\dfrac{16}{20} =$ _____

d $\dfrac{16}{64} =$ _____

4 Put the following fractions in order of size starting with the smallest:

a $\dfrac{1}{2}$, $\dfrac{1}{3}$, $\dfrac{4}{6}$ _____

b $\dfrac{2}{3}$, $\dfrac{4}{5}$, $\dfrac{6}{10}$ _____

> Even if you think you know the answer, you **must** show your workings.
> Look at question 4 on the help page and do the same here.
> In **a** change the fractions so they are all sixths (as 2, 3, and 6 will all go into 6).
> In **b** what number will 3, 5 and 10 all go into?

You need to know:

● How to change top heavy fractions to mixed numbers ● How to change mixed numbers to top heavy fraction

Remember: A mixed number is one where there are whole numbers and fractions.

EXAMPLE 1

Change $\frac{7}{3}$ (seven thirds) to a mixed number.

How many 3s go into 7?   **Answer**: 2 with 1 left over.

So, $\frac{7}{3}$ = = $2\frac{1}{3}$

EXAMPLE 2

Convert $\frac{17}{5}$ (seventeen fifths) to a mixed number.

How many 5s go into 17?   **Answer**: 3 with 2 left over.

So, $\frac{17}{5}$ = = $3\frac{2}{5}$

Remember: A top heavy fraction is one where the number at the top is bigger than the number at the bottom.

Question 1

Change these top heavy fractions into mixed numbers.

a $\frac{16}{7}$ How many 7s go into 16?   **Answer**: _____ with 2 left over.

So, $\frac{16}{7}$ = _____ $\frac{2}{7}$

b $\frac{18}{6}$ How many 6s go into 18?   **Answer**: _____ with 0 left over.

So, $\frac{18}{6}$ = _____

Fill in the blank spaces, to complete question 1 a and b.

Hint: Draw fraction diagrams if it helps, like the ones in the examples.

EXAMPLE 3

Change $2\frac{2}{3}$ to a top heavy fraction.

How many $\frac{1}{3}$s in a whole?   3, so 2 wholes x 3 = 6 then + 2 = 8

So, $2\frac{2}{3}$ = $\frac{8}{3}$ (or use a fraction diagram)

A quick way to change $2\frac{2}{3}$ is $2 \times 3 + 2 = 8$, so $2\frac{2}{3} = \frac{8}{3}$

Question 2

Change these mixed numbers into top heavy fractions:

a $8\frac{2}{3}$ 8 x 3 = _____ + 2 = _____   Answer: $8\frac{2}{3}$ = $\frac{}{3}$

b $1\frac{3}{8}$ ___ x 8 = ___ + 3 = ___   Answer: $1\frac{3}{8}$ = $\frac{}{8}$

Complete the workings and answers for question 2.

1 Change these top heavy (improper) fractions into mixed numbers.

a $\dfrac{3}{2} =$ _____   b $\dfrac{4}{2} =$ _____   c $\dfrac{5}{2} =$ _____

d $\dfrac{8}{3} =$ _____   e $\dfrac{9}{3} =$ _____   f $\dfrac{10}{3} =$ _____

g $\dfrac{13}{5} =$ _____   h $\dfrac{14}{5} =$ _____   i $\dfrac{15}{5} =$ _____

j $\dfrac{99}{10} =$ _____   k $\dfrac{100}{10} =$ _____   l $\dfrac{101}{10} =$ _____

2 Change the following mixed numbers into top heavy (improper) fractions:

a $2\dfrac{1}{2} =$ _____   b $3\dfrac{1}{2} =$ _____   c $4\dfrac{1}{2} =$ _____

d $2\dfrac{1}{3} =$ _____   e $3\dfrac{2}{3} =$ _____   f $4\dfrac{1}{3} =$ _____

g $8\dfrac{2}{3} =$ _____   h $7\dfrac{3}{4} =$ _____   i $6\dfrac{4}{5} =$ _____

j $5\dfrac{5}{6} =$ _____   k $4\dfrac{6}{7} =$ _____   l $3\dfrac{7}{8} =$ _____

3 Put a circle around the correct answer.

a $\dfrac{11}{2} =$ $6\dfrac{1}{2}$ $11\dfrac{1}{2}$ $5\dfrac{1}{2}$

b $\dfrac{17}{3} =$ $6\dfrac{1}{3}$ $5\dfrac{2}{3}$ $5\dfrac{1}{3}$

c $5\dfrac{3}{4} =$ $\dfrac{20}{4}$ $\dfrac{25}{4}$ $\dfrac{23}{4}$

d $10\dfrac{2}{3} =$ $\dfrac{32}{3}$ $\dfrac{31}{3}$ $\dfrac{30}{3}$

Decide which one of the three answers is the correct one and put a circle around it.

You need to know:
- How to find a fraction of an amount

EXAMPLE 1

Calculate each of these:

a $\frac{3}{5}$ of 35

Step 1: Find $\frac{1}{5}$ of 35 $35 \div 5 = 7$

Step 2: Find $\frac{3}{5}$ of 35 $3 \times 7 = 21$

b $\frac{5}{8}$ of 16

Step 1: Find $\frac{1}{8}$ of 16 $16 \div 8 = 2$

Step 2: Find $\frac{5}{8}$ of 16 $5 \times 2 = 10$

Remember: When finding a fraction of an amount, always divide the amount by the bottom of the fraction then times by the top.

EXAMPLE 2

Lee earns £500 a week. $\frac{3}{10}$ of his wages pay the rent. How much rent does he pay?

Step 1: Find $\frac{1}{10}$ of £500 $500 \div 10 = 50$

Step 2: Find $\frac{3}{10}$ of £500 $3 \times 50 = £150$

Example 2 is simply asking you to find $\frac{3}{10}$ of £500.

Remember: Units! This question uses £, so the answer must have the £ sign as well.

Question 1

Calculate each of these quantities:

a $\frac{3}{4}$ of 240 kg

Step 1: Find $\frac{1}{4}$ of 240 $240 \div 4 = \_\_\_$

Step 2: Find $\frac{3}{4}$ of 240 $3 \times \_\_\_ = \_\_\_$ kg

b $\frac{7}{8}$ of £32

Step 1: Find $\frac{1}{8}$ of 32 $32 \div 8 = \_\_\_$

Step 2: Find $\frac{7}{8}$ of 32 $\_\_\_ \times \_\_\_ = £ \_\_\_$

Complete the workings for question 1 **a** and **b**.

Hint: to quickly calculate 240÷4, do 24÷4 then add a zero to your answer.

Question 2

A special offer says: Chocolate biscuits 400 g packet + $\frac{1}{10}$ extra free!

a What is the weight of the extra free biscuits?
$\frac{1}{10}$ of 400 $400 \div \_\_\_ = \_\_\_$ g

b What is the total weight of the special offer packet?
Total weight = 400 g + ___ g = ___ g

Complete the workings for question 2.

Hint: For question 2**b**, to find the total weight, add your answer for **a** to the 400 g.

1 Find each of these:

a $\frac{1}{3}$ of 24 = _____

b $\frac{1}{4}$ of 24 = _____

c $\frac{1}{8}$ of 24 = _____

d $\frac{1}{5}$ of 30 = _____

e $\frac{1}{2}$ of 30 = _____

f $\frac{1}{10}$ of 30 = _____

2 Calculate each of these quantities:

a $\frac{2}{3}$ of 24 kg = _____

b $\frac{3}{4}$ of 24 g = _____

c $\frac{4}{5}$ of £30 = _____

d $\frac{7}{10}$ of 30 m = _____

Remember: Show all your workings and don't forget the units on your answer.

3 A special offer on a packet says: 500 g + $\frac{1}{5}$ extra free!

a What is the weight that is given for free? _____

b What is the total weight of the special offer packet? _____

4 A new stereo costing £280 is reduced by $\frac{1}{4}$ in a sale.

a Find $\frac{1}{4}$ of £280 _____

b How much does the stereo cost in the sale? _____

5 A woman left $\frac{2}{5}$ of her estate to her granddaughter.

If the estate total is £9600, how much does the granddaughter get? _____

_____

1 Write down what fraction of each of these shapes is shaded.

a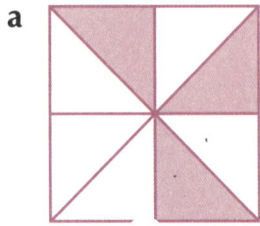

b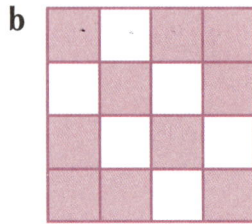

c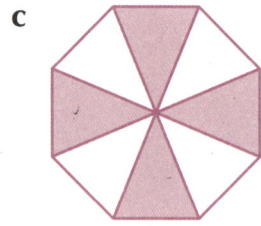

_____ 　 _____ 　 _____

2 Shade in the fraction given for each shape.

a $\dfrac{1}{4}$ 　　　 b $\dfrac{1}{4}$ 　　　 c $\dfrac{5}{6}$ 　　　 d $\dfrac{2}{5}$

 　  　 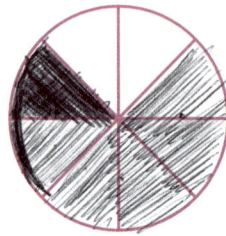 　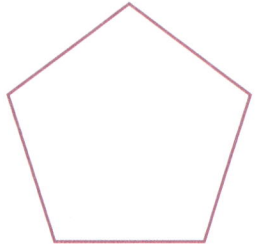

3 Find the answers to these fraction questions.

a $\dfrac{7}{12} + \dfrac{2}{12} =$ _____ 　　 b $\dfrac{8}{12} + \dfrac{2}{12} =$ _____ 　　 c $\dfrac{9}{12} - \dfrac{5}{12} =$ _____

4 Fill in the boxes with the equivalent fractions.

a $\dfrac{3}{7} = \dfrac{\square}{14} = \dfrac{9}{\square} = \dfrac{\square}{70}$ 　　　　 b $\dfrac{\square}{5} = \dfrac{8}{10} = \dfrac{40}{\square} = \dfrac{\square}{20}$

5 Cancel down these fractions to their simplest form.

a $\dfrac{6}{30} =$ _____ 　　 b $\dfrac{16}{30} =$ _____ 　　 c $\dfrac{6}{16} =$ _____

6 Put this list of fractions in order of size starting with the smallest.

$\dfrac{1}{4}$, 　 $\dfrac{2}{5}$, 　 $\dfrac{3}{10}$, 　 $\dfrac{4}{20}$, 　 _____

7 Change these improper fractions into mixed numbers:

a $\dfrac{5}{2} =$ _____   **b** $\dfrac{8}{2} =$ _____   **c** $\dfrac{8}{3} =$ _____   **d** $\dfrac{8}{5} =$ _____

8 Change these mixed numbers into improper fractions:

a $2\dfrac{1}{5} =$ _____   **b** $6\dfrac{2}{5} =$ _____   **c** $3\dfrac{3}{10} =$ _____   **d** $5\dfrac{21}{100} =$ _____

9 Find:

a $\dfrac{1}{3}$ of 15 = _____   **b** $\dfrac{1}{7}$ of 70 = _____   **c** $\dfrac{1}{10}$ of 70 = _____

10 Calculate:

a $\dfrac{2}{3}$ of £15 = _____   **b** $\dfrac{4}{7}$ of 70 kg = _____   **c** $\dfrac{7}{10}$ of 70 m = _____

11 Calculate:

a $\dfrac{3}{4}$ of £24 = _____   **b** $\dfrac{2}{5}$ of 45 kg = _____   **c** $\dfrac{3}{8}$ of 32 m = _____

12 A bike normally costs £300. In a sale it is sold for '$\dfrac{1}{3}$ off'.

a Find $\dfrac{1}{3}$ of £300 _____

b How much does the bike cost in the sale? _____

13 Which is the most: $\dfrac{1}{3}$ of £240, or $\dfrac{2}{5}$ of £180, and by how much?

_____

_____

You need to know:
- How to use negative numbers in everyday situations
- How to add and subtract negative numbers

EXAMPLE 1

Are the following statements True (**T**) or False (**F**)?

a 0 is bigger than -3 T

    0 is higher up the scale than -3

b -6 is smaller than -1 T

    -6 is lower down the scale than -1

c -6 is bigger than -4 F

    -6 is smaller/lower than -4 not bigger

d 0 is smaller than 4 T

    0 is lower than 4

Number line: 7, 6, 5, 4, 3, 2, 1, 0, -1, -2, -3, -4, -5, -6, -7

EXAMPLE 2

Work out the answers to the following questions:

a $2 - 4 =$ start at 2 on the number line, then count down 4 places -2

b $-2 - 4 =$ start at -2 on the number line, then count down 4 places -6

c $-4 + 2 =$ start at -4 on the number line, then count up 2 places -2

d $-2 - -4 = -2 + 4 =$ start at -2 on the number line, then count up 4 places 2

    $-$ and $-$ replace with $+$

Question 1

If $+2°C$ means $2°C$ above freezing point, then _____ means $2°C$ below freezing point.

Question 2

Answer True (**T**) or False (**F**) to the following statements.

a 3 is smaller than 6   _____   **b** -3 is smaller than -6 _____

c -3 is bigger than -4 _____   **d** 2 is smaller than -6 _____

Question 3

Put the correct symbol, $>$ or $<$ in the space provided. The first one has been done for you.

a $5 > 3$ **b** -4 ___ 3 **c** -5 ___ -4 **d** 3 ___ 0 **e** 0 ___ -5

Question 4

Work out the answers to the following questions:

a $6 - 7 =$ start at 6 on the number line, then count down 7 places $=$ ___

b $-2 - 2 =$ start at -2 on the number line, then count down 2 places $=$ ___

c $-20 - 20 =$ start at -20 on the number line, then count down 20 places $=$ ___

d $-3 + -2 = -3$ ___ $2 =$ ___   **e** $2 - -5 = 2$ ___ $5 =$ ___

    $+$ and $-$ replace with $-$ $-$ and $-$ replace with ?

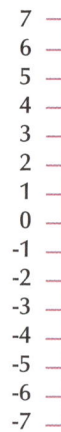

Hint: To help you answer questions with negative numbers, use a number line like the one on the left.

Remember: The higher the number is up the scale the bigger it is; the lower down the scale the smaller it is.

Remember: When two signs are together, use the following rules:

$+$ and $+$ replace with $+$
$+$ and $-$ replace with $-$
$-$ and $+$ replace with $-$
$-$ and $-$ replace with $+$

Fill in the blank space to make the sentence correct.

Write **T** for True or **F** for False in the spaces given - use the number line above to help you.

Remember:
$>$ means 'is bigger than'
$<$ means 'is smaller than'

Complete the workings for question 4; use the number line to help you when you can.

1 Complete each of the following:

    a If + £100 means a profit of one hundred pounds, then _____ means a loss of one hundred pounds.

    b If −20 °C means twenty degrees below freezing point, then + 20 °C means twenty degrees _____ freezing point.

> **Hint:** You can use the same number more than once if you want to.

2 Write one number from the following list:

$$-5 \qquad -1 \qquad 0 \qquad 2 \qquad 7$$

in the blank spaces below, to make the statements correct.

    a _____ is smaller than −1   **b** _____ is bigger than 2   **c** −6 is smaller than _____

    d −4 > _____   **e** 2< _____   **f** 0 > _____

3 Work out each of the following:

    a 4 °C − 6 °C = _____ °C   **b** 3 °F − 10 °F = _____ °F

    c − 2 °C + 7 °C = _____ °C   **d** − 4 °F − 3 °F = _____ °F

    e − 6 − 6 = _____   **f** − 10 − 10 = _____

    g 3 − (− 4) = _____   **h** − 4 − (− 3) = _____

    i 2 + (− 7) = _____   **j** − 7 + (− 2) = _____

4 What numbers are missing from the boxes to make the sums true?

    a 3 − ☐ = −1   **b** −5 + ☐ = 2

    c −8 + ☐ = −3   **d** 2 + (−6) = ☐

5 Draw a line connecting the question on the left with its correct answer on the right.

    a −7 − 2 + 5 =   **i** 4

    b 4 + 5 − 11 =   **ii** 2

    c 6 − (−3) − 5 =   **iii** −4

    d 7 + (−2) − 3 =   **iv** −2

You need to know:
- What a multiple is • What a factor is, and be able to find common factors of numbers
- What a prime number is, and be able to remember at least the first 10 prime numbers

EXAMPLE 1

What are the first five multiples of 3?

Answer: 3, 6, 9, 12, 15

EXAMPLE 2

Give the largest multiple of 9 which is less than 50?

The multiples of 9 are 9, 18, 27, 36, 45, 54, 63…

Answer: 45

Question 1

What are the first 4 multiples of 10?   **Answer:** _____, _____, _____, _____

Question 2

Give the largest multiple of 5 which is less than 50.

The multiples of 5 are 5, 10, 15, 20…   **Answer:** _____

EXAMPLE 3

What are the factors of 10?

$1 \times 10 = 10$; $2 \times 5 = 10$; so 1, 10, 2, 5 are the factors, but we usually write them in order of size

Answer: 1, 2, 5, 10

EXAMPLE 4

List all the factors of 16.

$1 \times 16 = 16$; $2 \times 8 = 16$; $4 \times 4 = 16$; so 1, 16, 2, 8, 4 are the factors

Answer: 1, 2, 4, 8, 16

Question 3

Find all the factors of 25.   **Answer:** _____, _____, _____

Question 4

Find all the factors of 40.   **Answer:** _____, _____, _____, _____,
_____, _____, _____, _____

Question 5

What factors are the common factors of 25 and 40?

Answer: _____ and _____

EXAMPLE 5

List the first 10 prime numbers.   **Answer:** 2, 3, 5, 7, 11, 13, 17, 19, 23, 29

Question 6

Write down the factors of the following numbers:

a 2 **Answer:** 1, 2   b 3 **Answer:** _____, _____   c 5 **Answer:** _____, _____

d 7 **Answer:** _____, _____

Question 7

How many factors has a prime number got? _____

Remember: **Multiples** of a number are just the times tables of that number.

45 is the **largest** multiple of 9 which is **less** than 50.

Give the first 4 numbers in the 10 times table.

Carry on the multiples of 5 list, then choose your answer, **but** it is not 50 as the answer must be **less than 50.**

Remember: A **factor** of a number is a number which will divide into that number exactly.

Fill in the blanks in these questions. Always start by writing the factors out in their pairs e.g. 1×40, 2×20 etc. then put them in order of size.

Which two numbers are in both factor lists?

A **prime** number can only be divided by itself and 1, no other number will divide exactly into it.

Fill in the blanks.

Use your answers to question 6 to help you answer question 7.

1 Write down the first 6 multiples of 8. _____

2 What is the largest multiple of 4 that is smaller than 25?

_____

Hint: Start listing the multiples of 4, then stop when you get to the one you want.

3 Transfer the numbers from the circle into the correct columns in the table. You can put some of the numbers in more than one column.

10 8 12
30 20
6 15 18
16 50
100 33 24

Multiple of 3	Multiple of 4	Multiple of 5	Multiple of 6

4 List all the factors of:

a 24 _____

b 36 _____

c What are the common factors of 24 and 36? _____

5 Use your calculator to find all the factors of:

a 140 _____

b 96 _____

c What are the common factors of 140 and 96? _____

6 Circle the numbers in the following list that are prime numbers:

5   21   37   13   26   32   11   111   39   47

You need to know:

- How to work out square numbers, square roots and powers ● The square numbers from 1^2 to 15^2

EXAMPLE 1

Without a calculator, work out the first 5 square numbers.

$1 \times 1 = 1$ $2 \times 2 = 4$ $3 \times 3 = 9$ $4 \times 4 = 16$ $5 \times 5 = 25$

Answer: 1, 4, 9, 16, 25

> **Remember:** To find the square of a number simply multiply the number by itself.

EXAMPLE 2

What is 6 squared?

6 squared = 6 × 6   **Answer:** = 36

EXAMPLE 3

What is 7^2?

$7^2 = 7 \times 7$ **Answer:** = 49

> **Remember:** All these are different ways of writing the square of 5:
> 5 squared = 5^2 = $5 \times 5 = 25$

Question 1

Without a calculator, work out the first 10 square numbers.

$1 \times 1 = 1$ $2 \times 2 = 4$ $3 \times 3 = 9 \ldots$

Answer: 1, 4, 9, ___, ___, ___, ___, ___, ___, ___

> Continue the pattern and fill in the blanks - the first three have been done for you.

Question 2

Calculate 20^2 **Answer:** $20^2 = 20 \times$ ___ = ___

> Complete the calculation.

EXAMPLE 4

What is the square root of 25?

what × what = 25?

$5 \times 5 = 25$ **Answer:** 5

EXAMPLE 5

Find the square root of 81.

what × what = 81?

$9 \times 9 = 81$ **Answer:** 9

> **Remember:** The square root is the reverse of squaring.
> $\sqrt{}$ is the symbol for square root.

EXAMPLE 6

Find $\sqrt{36}$.   **what × what = 36?** $6 \times 6 = 36$ **Answer:** 6

Question 3

Find the square root of 100.

what × what = 100?

___ × ___ = 100   **Answer:** ___

Question 4

Find $\sqrt{16}$.

what × what = 16?

___ × ___ = 16   **Answer:** ___

> Fill in the blanks.

EXAMPLE 7

Without using a calculator, find the value of 2^3.

2^3 means 2 × 2 × 2

$2 \times 2 = 4$, $4 \times 2 = 8$

Answer: 8

EXAMPLE 8

Using a calculator, find the value of 3^4.

3^4 means $3 \times 3 \times 3 \times 3 = 81$

Answer: 81

> **Remember:**
> 3^2 we say '3 squared'
> 3^3 we say '3 cubed'
> 3^4 we say '3 to the power of 4'
> 3^5 we say '3 to the power of 5'

Question 5

Use a calculator to find each of the following:

a 10^4 $10^4 =$ ___ × ___ × ___ × ___ = ___   **Answer:** ___

b 2^6 $2^6 =$ ___ × ___ × ___ × ___ × ___ × ___ = ___   **Answer:** ___

c 11^3 $11^3 =$ ___ × ___ × ___ = ___   **Answer:** ___

> Fill in the blanks in the workings to find the answers.

Answer questions 1 and 2 without using a calculator.

1 Cover up the help page so that you try this question with no help.
Write down the first 12 square numbers:

> **Remember:** the first one is $1 \times 1 = 1$

_____

2 What are the values of these?

> **Hint:** Use your answers to question 1 to help.

a 7 squared = _____

b 10 squared = _____

c 8^2 = _____

d square root of 81 = _____

e $\sqrt{16}$ = _____

f $\sqrt{36}$ = _____

3 Use a calculator to work out the following:

a 30^2 = _____

b 20^3 = _____

c 15^4 = _____

d 10^5 = _____

e 5^5 = _____

f 2^{10} = _____

g 1^{20} = _____

h 6^4 = _____

i $\sqrt{1225}$ = _____

j $\sqrt{2025}$ = _____

k $\sqrt{3025}$ = _____

l $\sqrt{4225}$ = _____

m $\sqrt{5625}$ = _____

n $\sqrt{7225}$ = _____

o $\sqrt{9025}$ = _____

p $\sqrt{625}$ = _____

4 Transfer the numbers from the circle into the correct columns in the table.
You can put some of the numbers in more than one column.

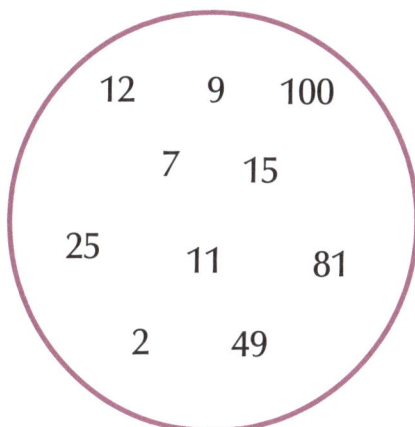

12   9   100
7   15
25   11   81
2   49

Odd number	Even number	Square number	Prime number

You need to know:
- How to work out the area of a rectangle
- How to estimate the area of an irregular shape

EXAMPLE 1

Calculate the area of the following rectangle:

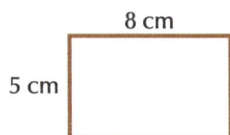

8 cm
5 cm

$$\text{Area} = \text{length} \times \text{width}$$
$$= 8 \times 5$$
$$= 40 \text{ cm}^2$$

Remember: Area of a rectangle = length × width or base × height or up × across. It doesn't matter which one you use, but make sure you use one of them!

Question 1

Calculate the area of the following rectangles:

a 10 mm 2 mm

$$\text{Area} = \text{length} \times \text{width}$$
$$= 10 \times \underline{\quad}$$
$$= \underline{\quad} \text{ mm}^2$$

b 4 m 3 m

$$\text{Area} = \underline{\quad} \times \underline{\quad}$$
$$= \underline{\quad} \times \underline{\quad}$$
$$= 12 \text{ m}^2$$

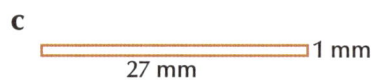

c 1 mm 27 mm

$$\text{Area} = \underline{\quad} \times \underline{\quad}$$
$$= \underline{\quad} \times \underline{\quad}$$
$$= \underline{\quad} \text{ mm}^2$$

Complete the workings and answers for question 1.

Hint: In the GCSE you must always quote a formula before you use it.

Remember: Units for area are always something^2 e.g. mm^2, cm^2, m^2, km^2

EXAMPLE 2

Estimate the area of the shape below.

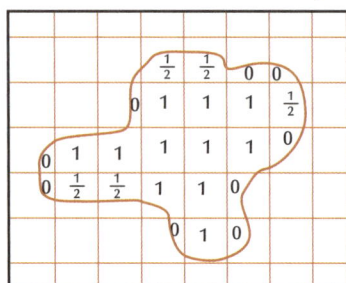

When estimating:
- count all complete and nearly complete squares as 1,
- count all $\frac{1}{2}$ squares as $\frac{1}{2}$,
- count all squares less than $\frac{1}{2}$ as 0

$$\text{Area} = 11 + \frac{1}{2} + \frac{1}{2} + \frac{1}{2} + \frac{1}{2} + \frac{1}{2}$$
$$= 13\frac{1}{2} \text{ cm}^2$$

Hint: Estimate means give a rough answer - you're not expected to work out the accurate answer.

Question 2

Estimate the area of the shapes below.

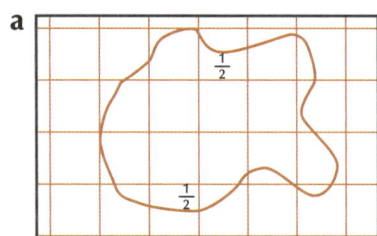

a

$$\text{Area} = \underline{\quad} + \frac{1}{2} + \frac{1}{2} = \underline{\quad} \text{ cm}^2$$

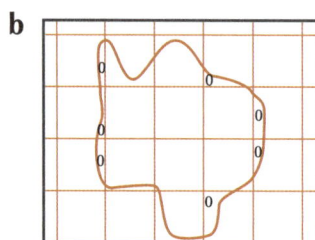

b

$$\text{Area} = \underline{\qquad} = \underline{\quad} \text{ cm}^2$$

Complete question 2. In **a** you need to write on the shape all the 1s and 0s and find the total area. In **b** you need to write on the shape all the 1s and $\frac{1}{2}$ s and find the total area.

1. Work out the area of the following shapes.

Each square on the grid is 1 cm². Count the squares to find the area.

a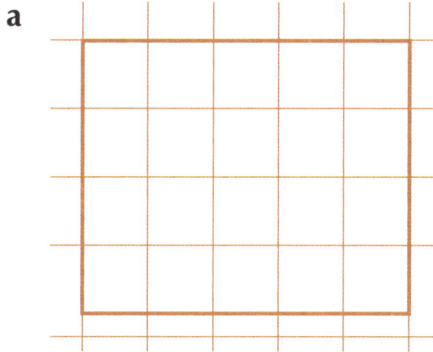

b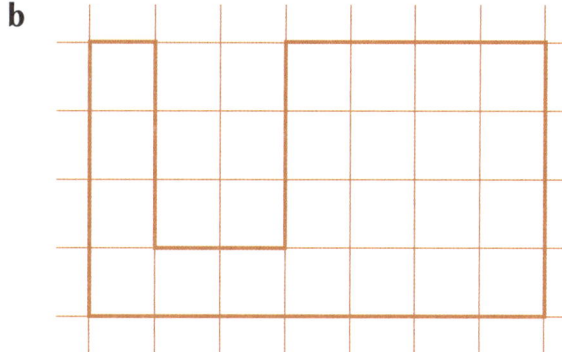

Area = _____ cm²

Area = _____ cm²

2. Calculate the area of these rectangles.

a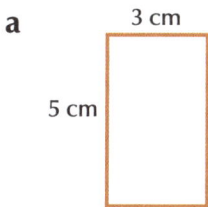
3 cm
5 cm

b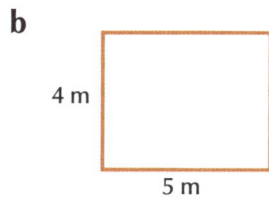
4 m
5 m

c
17 mm
1 mm

Area = _____

Area = _____

Area = _____

Don't forget the units in your answers.

3. The map below shows a small island. Each square on the map represents 1 km². Estimate the area of the island.

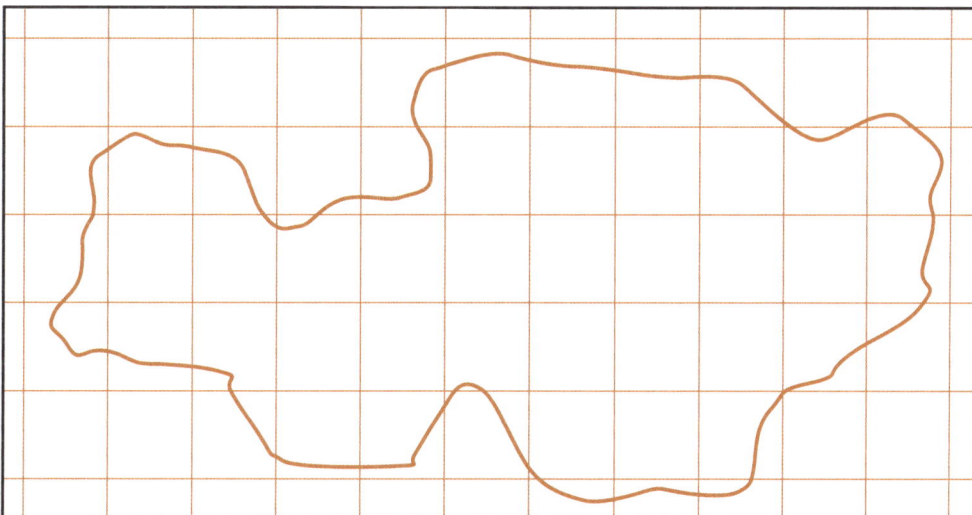

Area = _____

1 Fill in the missing word.

If +13 °C means 13 degrees above freezing, then −13 °C means 13 degrees _____ freezing.

2 Use a number from this list to fill in the blank spaces. (You can use the same number more than once.)

$$-6 \qquad -3 \qquad 0 \qquad 4 \qquad 6$$

a _____ is smaller than −4   **b** _____ is bigger than 4

c −5 is smaller than _____   **d** $0 >$ _____   **e** $3 <$ _____

3 Fill in the box for each question.

a $3\,°C - 6\,°C = \boxed{}$ **b** $-6 - (-2) = \boxed{}$ **c** $4 - \boxed{} = -1$

d $3 - \boxed{} = 5$ **e** $2 + (-4) = \boxed{}$ **f** $-7 - (-2) + 4 = \boxed{}$

4 List the first 5 multiples of 6. _____

5 Which is the biggest multiple of 7 that is less than 50? _____

6 List the factors of 18. _____

7 List the factors of 27. _____

8 What are the common factors of 18 and 27? _____

9 Use your calculator to find all the factors of 150. _____

38

10 Write down 10 prime numbers. _____

11 Write down the first 10 square numbers. _____

12 Without a calculator, find the value of the following:

a 4 squared = _____   b 6^2 = _____   c $\sqrt{100}$ = _____

d the square root of 64 = _____   e $2 \times 2 \times 2$ = _____

13 With a calculator, find the value of the following:

a 17^2 = _____   b 17^3 = _____   c 17^4 = _____

d 3^{10} = _____   e 10^3 = _____   f $\sqrt{784}$ = _____

g $\sqrt{841}$ = _____   h $\sqrt{900}$ = _____

14 Find the area of these five shapes.

a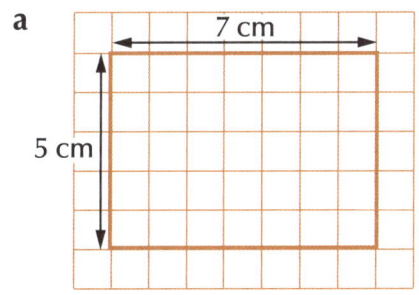

Area = _____ cm^2

b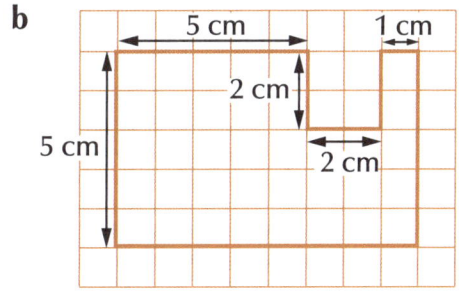

Area = _____ cm^2

c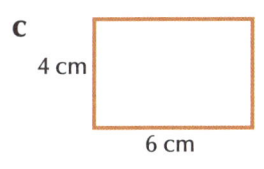

Area = _____ cm^2

d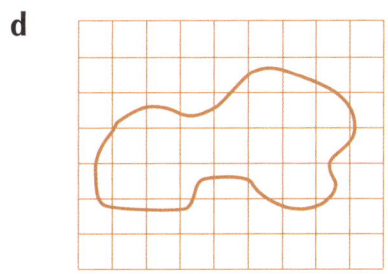

Area = _____ cm^2

e

Area = _____ cm^2

You need to know:

● How to work out the perimeter of a shape

EXAMPLE 1

Find the perimeter of the following rectangle:

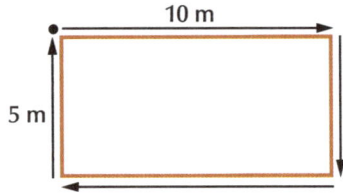

To find the perimeter, decide where to start and 'travel' around the edge of the shape.

$P = 10 + 5 + 10 + 5 = 30$ m

> **Remember:** The perimeter of a shape is the total distance around the edge of the shape

> **Remember:** Units for perimeter are simply mm, cm, m, km

Question 1

Find the perimeter of the following rectangles:

a

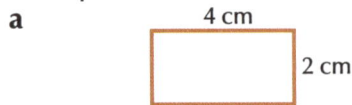

$P = \underline{\quad} + \underline{\quad} + \underline{\quad} + \underline{\quad} = 12$ cm

b

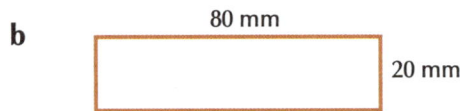

$P = 80 + 20 + \underline{\quad} + \underline{\quad} = \underline{\quad}$ mm

> Fill in the blank spaces to complete question 1

EXAMPLE 2

Find the perimeter of this 'L' shape:

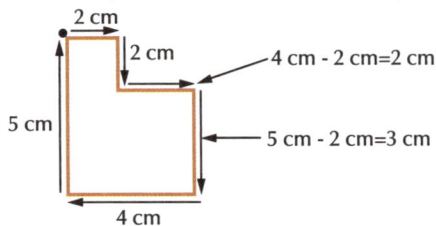

Before we can find the perimeter, we need to find the lengths of all the sides.

$P = 2 + 2 + 2 + 3 + 4 + 5 = 18$ cm

> **Hint:** Use the given measurements to find the lengths of the sides you don't know.

Question 2

Find the perimeters of these unusual shapes.

a

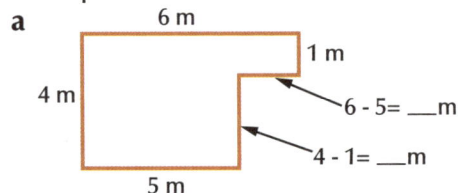

$P = 6 + 1 + \underline{\quad} + \underline{\quad} + 5 + 4 = \underline{\quad}$ m

b

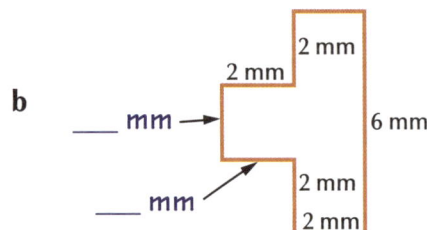

> Find the lengths of the sides shown by the arrows, then complete the workings to find the perimeters.

$P = \underline{\quad} + \underline{\quad} + \underline{\quad} + \underline{\quad} + \underline{\quad} + \underline{\quad} + \underline{\quad} + \underline{\quad} = \underline{\quad}$ mm

1 Work out the perimeter of the following shapes.

Each square on the grid is 1 cm by 1 cm.

a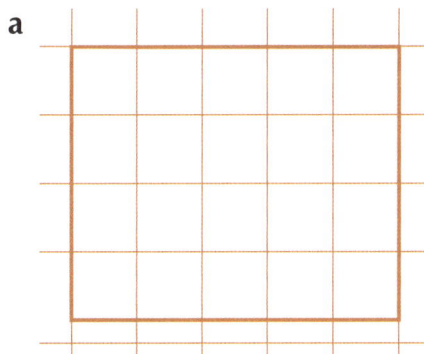

Perimeter = _____ cm

b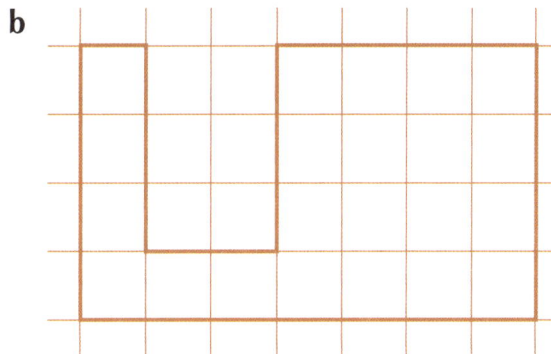

Perimeter = _____ cm

2 Calculate the perimeter of these rectangles.

a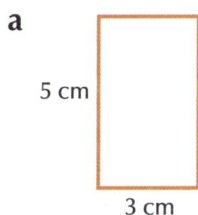

5 cm

3 cm

Perimeter = _____

b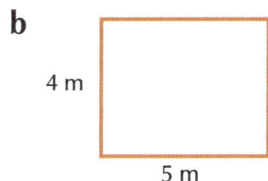

4 m

5 m

Perimeter = _____

c

17 mm

1 mm

Perimeter = _____

Don't forget the units on your answers

3 Mr Williams wants to put a small fence all the way around his vegetable plot. A diagram of the plot is shown below.

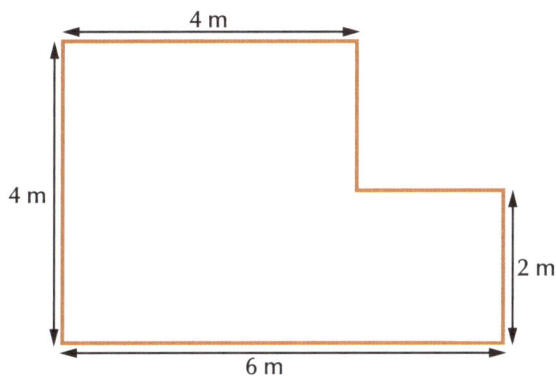

4 m

4 m

2 m

6 m

What is the total length of fence he needs?

_____

You need to know:

● How to draw frequency tables, pictograms and bar charts

EXAMPLE 1

Dai kept a record of the number of text messages his friends sent him over a period of 3 weeks.

	Week 1						
Day	Sun	Mon	Tue	Wed	Thu	Fri	Sat
Number of text messages	2	4	2	6	1	5	4

	Week 2						
Day	Sun	Mon	Tue	Wed	Thu	Fri	Sat
Number of text messages	3	3	2	3	2	1	6

	Week 3						
Day	Sun	Mon	Tue	Wed	Thu	Fri	Sat
Number of text messages	3	3	4	5	1	6	3

a Draw a frequency table for all of this data.
b Draw a pictogram for week 1.
c Draw a bar chart for week 2.

a

Number of texts	Tally	Frequency
1	I I	
2	I I I I	4
3	I I I	
4	I I	
5	I	
6	I I	

This shows there were 4 days when Dai had 2 text messages

So far the pictogram shows us there were:
2 messages on Sunday (1 phone)
4 on Monday (2 phones)
only 1 on Thursday ($\frac{1}{2}$ a phone)

b

Sun	✆
Mon	✆✆
Tue	
Wed	
Thur	◗
Fri	
Sat	

Key: ✆ = 2 text messages

c

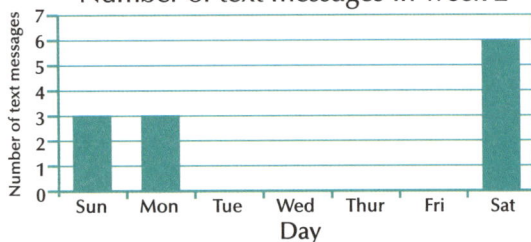

Number of text messages in week 2

Sunday, Monday and Saturday have already been done

Remember:
When drawing a tally chart, every 5th tally crosses the previous 4, to make blocks of 5: ⊔⊦⊦⊦

Remember:
The frequency is found by adding up the tallies.

Complete the tally and frequency columns - the first 2 weeks have already been tallied up.

Remember:
A pictogram must always have a key to show what each 'picture' is worth.

Complete the pictogram – Sunday, Monday and Thursday have already been done for you.

Remember:
A bar chart should always have bars the same width, and the gap between the bars should be the same size.

Complete the bar chart.

1 Mr Davies plants 20 seeds. One month after planting the seeds, he measures the heights of the seedlings in centimetres. The heights are:

7 9 7 11 6 10 9 8 8 7 8 7 6 7 11 8 8 9 10 6

a Complete the frequency table below for this data.

Height in cm	Tally	Frequency
6		
7		
8		
9		
10		
11		

b Draw a pictogram for this data.

Use the key: ☀ = 2 plants

6	
7	
8	
9	
10	
11	

Hint: Use the frequency column from part **a** to help with **b** and **c**

c Draw a bar chart for this data.

Heights in seedlings

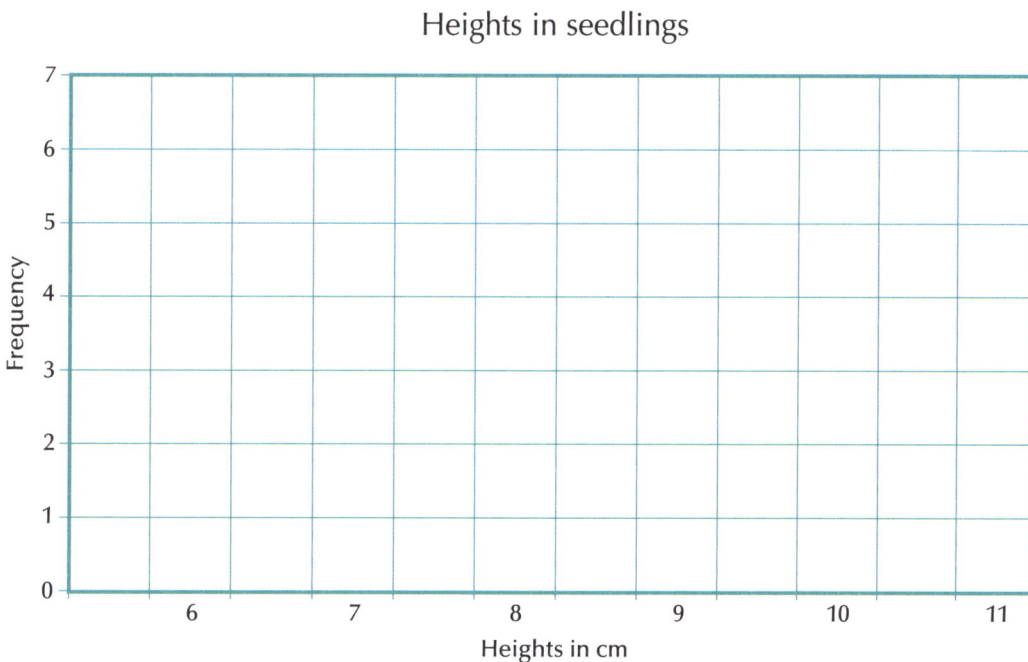

You need to know:
- How to collect data
- How to read and interpret pictograms and barcharts

EXAMPLE 1

Draw a line between the type of data that needs to be collected and the method of sampling.

DATA NEEDED	METHOD OF SAMPLING
Favourite TV programme of teacher	Take a sample
How often a two occurs when a dice is rolled	Observation
How many blue cars there are in the school car park	Experiment

Question 1

The pictogram shows the average daily rainfall in Snowdonia over 5 months.

November	☁☁☁
December	☁☁☁☁
January	☁☁☁☁☁
February	☁☁☁☁
March	☁☁

Key: ☁ = 1 mm

a Which month had the highest average daily rainfall? _____

b What was the average daily rainfall in December? _____

c Which month had an average daily rainfall of 3 mm? _____

Question 2

The bar chart shows the favourite colours of some students.

Favourite colours of students

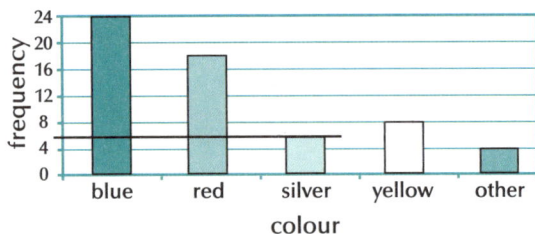

a How many students' favourite colour was silver? _____

b How many students were asked their favourite colour? _____

Sidebar notes:

What is your teacher's favourite TV programme? You would have to ask them, so draw a line to 'Take a sample'.

How often does a 2 occur when a dice is rolled? You would have to roll it, so draw a line to 'Experiment'.

How many blue cars are in the car park? You would have to go and look, so draw a line to 'Observation'.

Hint: If ☁ = 1 mm of rain, then ☁ = ½ mm of rain

Remember: Most rain clouds = most rain!

Use the pictogram to answer these questions.

Hint: 3 mm = ☁☁☁

Remember: In this chart the frequency is the number of students.

In **a**, draw a line across from the bar to the scale to help you read the number.

Add up all the bars to get the answer to **b**.

1 Circle the method you would use to collect data for the following surveys:

a How many times a coin lands on heads when it is thrown?

    Experiment   Observation   Take a sample

b Who is the favourite film star of students in your year group?

    Experiment   Observation   Take a sample

c How many car parking spaces are not used in the school car park?

    Experiment   Observation   Take a sample

2 Lynn wants to go to the Grand Canyon in America. She sees this information in a book, showing the average daily sunshine in 4 different months:

April	✿ ✿ ✿ ✿ ✿
July	✿ ✿ ✿ ✿ ✿ ◖
October	✿ ✿ ✿ ✿ ◖
January	✿ ✿ ✿ ✿

Key: ✿ = 2 hours

a Which month had the most daily sunshine? _____

b What was the average daily sunshine in January? _____

c Which month has an average daily sunshine of 9 hours? _____

3 As part of a 'Leisure and Tourism' survey, Carly asked her friends what their favourite sport to watch on TV was. This bar chart shows her results.

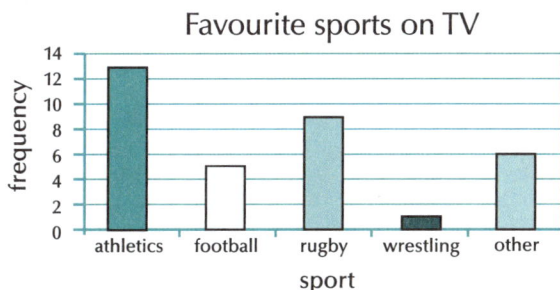

Favourite sports on TV

a How many of Carly's friends favourite sport was rugby? _____

b How many friends did Carly ask altogether? _____

You need to know:
● How to form algebraic expressions

EXAMPLE 1

Write down the algebraic expression that says:

a 4 more than x
'4 more than' is the same as '+4'   **Answer:** x + 4

b 2 less than q
'2 less than' is the same as '−2'   **Answer:** q − 2

c 3 divided by a
'3 ÷ a' is usually written as a fraction   **Answer:** $\frac{3}{a}$

d t multiplied by t
$t \times t = t^2$ **Answer:** t^2

Question 1

Circle the correct expression for each statement.

a 5 less than a   5 − a   (a − 5)   −5 − a
b b more than a   a + b   a − b   ab
c c multiplied by itself   c + c   2 × c c^2
d d divided by e $\frac{e}{d}$ $\frac{d}{e}$ e ÷ d

EXAMPLE 2

Quad bikes have 4 wheels. Which of the following rules connects the number of wheels (W) to the number of bikes (B)?

W + B = 4   ✗   (number of wheels + number of bikes = 4)
B = 4W   ✗   (number of bikes = 4 x number of wheels)
W = 4 + B   ✗   (number of wheels = 4 + number of bikes)
W = 4B   ✓   (number of wheels = 4 × number of bikes)

Question 2

Amy, Brett and Carla are friends. Brett is **y** years old.
Amy is 2 years older than Brett, and Carla is a year younger than Brett.
Draw a line linking each friend to their correct age, and cross out any unused answers.

Amy   Brett   Carla

y - 2   y   y + 1   3y   y - 1
2y   y + 2   y + 3

1 Write down the algebraic expression that says:

a 10 more than x = _____

b y more than x = _____

c 10 less than x = _____

d y less than x = _____

e 10 divided by x = _____

f y divided by x = _____

g 10 multiplied by x = _____

h y multiplied by x = _____

i x multiplied by itself = _____

j y multiplied by y = _____

2 This square has a side of length **a** cm.

a What is the perimeter of the square? _____

b What is the area of the square? _____

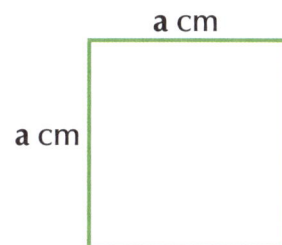

a cm

a cm

3 Lomu, Whoopee and Cleo are 3 dogs. Cleo is **x** years old.
Lomu is 5 years older than Cleo, and Whoopee is 2 years younger than Cleo.
Draw a line linking each dog to their correct age, and cross out any unused answers.

Lomu	Whoopee	Cleo
x − 5	5x	x + 7
x − 2	2x	x − 2
x + 5	x	x + 2

4 There are 100 cm in one metre.
A rule which connects the number of centimetres (C) with the number of metres (M) is: $C = 100M$

Write down a rule, using the letters shown which connects:

a the total number of legs (L) on (H) horses _____

b the total number of arms (A) on (O) octopi _____

c the total number of corners (C) on (T) triangles _____

d the total number of sides (S) on (P) pentagons _____

e the total number of millimetres (M) in (C) centimetres _____

1 Find the perimeter of these 5 shapes.

a

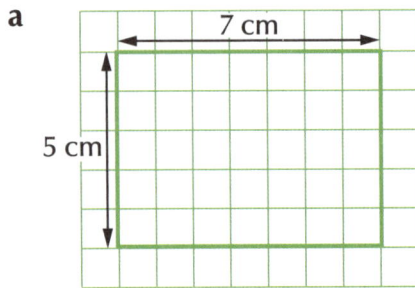

Perimeter = _____ cm

b

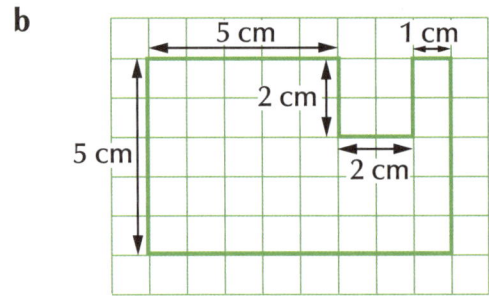

Perimeter = _____ cm

c

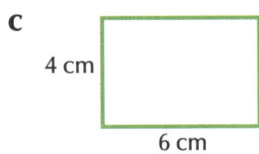

Perimeter = _____ cm

d

Perimeter = _____ cm

e

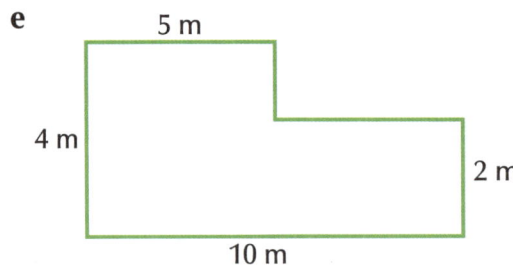

Perimeter = _____ m

2 **a** Mr Jones wants to collect data about the height of his seedlings, one month after he plants 20 seeds. Put a circle around the method he would use:

Experiment   **Observation**   **Take a sample**

The actual heights of his seedlings in cm are:

11, 13, 11, 15, 10, 14, 13, 12, 12, 11, 12, 11, 10, 11, 15, 12, 12, 13, 14, 10

b Complete the frequency table for this data:

Height in cm	Tally	Frequency
10		
11		
12		
13		
14		
15		

c Draw a pictogram for this data.

Height in cm	Key: ✳ = 2 seedlings
10	
11	
12	
13	
14	
15	

d In a gardening magazine, Mr Jones sees a bar chart showing the heights of the same type of seedlings, one month after planting.

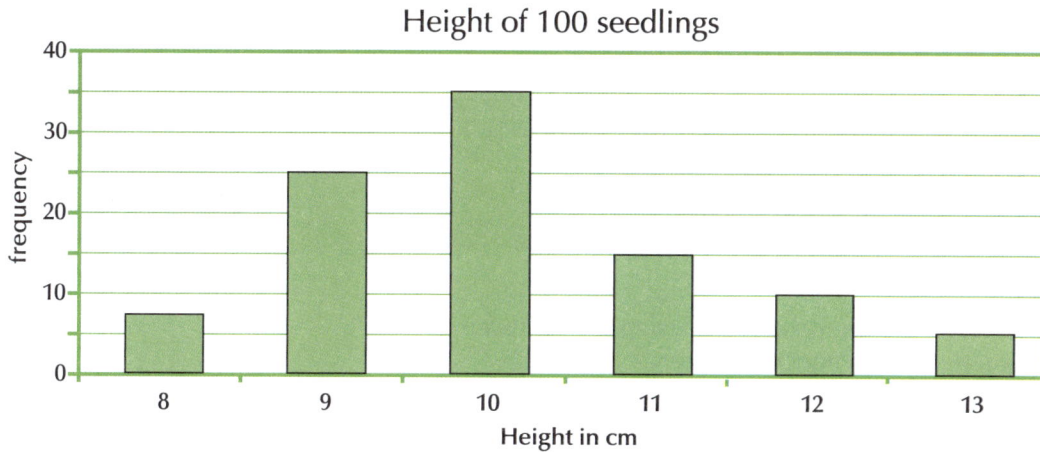

Height of 100 seedlings

i How many plants in the magazine were 10 cm tall? _____

ii How many plants in the magazine were taller than 10 cm? _____

3 Write down the algebraic expression that says:

a 3 more than x = _____   **b** 9 less than y = _____

c y divided by p = _____   **d** p multiplied by itself = _____

4 This rectangle has one side length **a**, and another side length **b**.

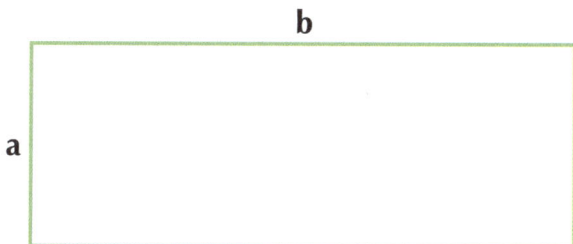

Draw a line connecting the area and perimeter to their correct expressions.

2**a** + 2**b**

area

2 × **a** × 2 × **b**

a × **b**

2 × **a** × **b**

perimeter

2 + **a** + 2 + **b**

a × **b** × **a** × **b**

You need to know:
- How to substitute numbers into formulae
- How to recognise patterns in number sequences

EXAMPLE 1

What is the area of a rectangle with a length of 6 cm and a width of 4 cm?

The formula for the area of a rectangle is:
Area = length × width

Answer: Area = $6 \times 4 = 24 \text{ cm}^2$

EXAMPLE 2

Find the cost when the cement mixer is hired for 8 hours.

The cost, in pounds, of hiring a cement mixer is given by the formula:
Cost = number of hours × 8 + 20

Answer: Cost = 8 × 8 + 20
= 64 + 20 = £84

> **Hint:** Just substitute the numbers into the formula, then work it out.

> **Remember:** BODMAS from chapter 1? × must be done before +

Question 1

Find the cost when the cement mixer in Example 2 is hired for 12 hours.

Cost = ____ × 8 + 20 = ____ + 20 = £____

> Fill in the blank spaces to complete question 1.

EXAMPLE 3

Find the total cost for a family of 2 adults and 2 children.

The total cost, in pounds, for a boat trip is found using the formula:
Cost 5 number of adults × 15 + number of children × 10

Answer: Cost = 2 × 15 + 2 × 10 = 30 + 20 = **£50**

Question 2

Find the total cost for the boat trip in Example 3 for a family of 1 adult and 3 children.

Answer: Cost = ____ × 15 + ____ × 10 = 15 + ____ = £____

> Complete question 2.

EXAMPLE 4

Find the perimeter of a square of side length 8 cm.

The formula for the perimeter of a square is: P = 4w where w is the width of the square.

Answer: P = 4 × 8 = **32** cm

> **Remember:** 4w means 4 × w

Question 3

Find the perimeter of a square of side length 10 cm.

Answer: = P = 4 × ____ = ____ cm

> Complete question 3.

EXAMPLE 5

Look at the following number sequences.
Write down the next two terms in each, and explain how each sequence is found.

a 5, 7, 9, 11   **Answer:** 13, 15   **Rule:** +2 each time
b 2, 4, 8, 16   **Answer:** 32, 64   **Rule:** ×2 each time

Question 4

Look at the following number sequences.
Write down the next two terms in each, and explain how each sequence is found.

a 16, 14, 12, 10, ____, ____   **Rule:** −2 each time
b 1, 3, 9, 27, ____, ____   **Rule:** ____

> Complete the answers for question 4.

1 A formula for estimating the perimeter of a circular pond is:

Perimeter = 3 × diameter

a What is the perimeter of a pond with a diameter of 4 m? _____

b What is the perimeter of a pond with a diameter of 6 m? _____

2 The formula for finding the cost (in pounds) of repairing a dishwasher is:

Cost = 20 × number of hours + 30

a What is the cost of repairing the dishwasher if it takes 1 hour to fix? _____

b What is the cost of repairing the dishwasher if it takes 3 hours to fix? _____

3 The formula for finding the total cost in pounds of entry to the zoo for adults and children is:

T = 20 × number of adults + 15 × number of children

a What is the total cost for a family of 1 adult and 2 children? _____

b What is the total cost for a family of 2 adults and 3 children? _____

4 The formula for finding the perimeter of a triangle with sides of length a, b, and c is:

P = a + b + c

a What is the perimeter of a triangle when a = 3 cm, b = 4 cm, and c = 5 cm? _____

b What is the perimeter of a triangle when a = 12 m, b = 6 m, and c = 9 m? _____

5 Look at the following number sequences. Write down the next three terms in each one, and the rule for finding the sequence:

a 4, 7, 10, 13, _____, _____, _____   **Rule:** _____

b 3, 6, 12, 24, _____, _____, _____   **Rule:** _____

c 5, 15, 25, 35, _____, _____, _____   **Rule:** _____

d 36, 30, 24, 18, _____, _____, _____   **Rule:** _____

e 160, 80, 40, 20, _____, _____, _____   **Rule:** _____

f 40 000, 4000, 400, _____, _____, _____   **Rule:** _____

You need to know:

- How to round decimal numbers to the nearest whole number
- How to round decimal numbers to 1, 2, and 3 decimal places

EXAMPLE 1

Round 31.7592 to:

a   the nearest whole number.

> 31.**7** is between 31 and 32, but which is closer?

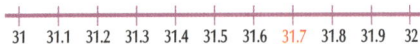

31   31.1   31.2   31.3   31.4   31.5   31.6   31.7   31.8   31.9   32

Answer: 32

b   1 decimal place.

> 31.7**5** is between 31.7 and 31.8, but which is closer?

> It is exactly half way, so round up

31.7   31.71   31.72   31.73   31.74   31.75   31.76   31.77   31.78   31.79   31.8

Answer: 31.8

c   2 decimal places.

> 31.75**9** is between 31.75 and 31.76, but which is closer?

31.75   31.752   31.754   31.756   31.758   31.76

Answer: 31.76

d   3 decimal places.

> 31.759**2** is between 31.759 and 31.760, but which is closer?

31.759   31.7592   31.7594   31.7596   31.7598   31.760

Answer: 31.759

Question 1

Round 5.961 to the nearest whole number. 5.**9** is between 5 and 6, but which is closer?

Answer: _____

Question 2

Round 0.173 to 1 decimal place. 0.1**7** is between 0.1 and 0.2, but which is closer?

Answer: _____

Question 3

Round 9.375 to 2 decimal places. 9.37**5** is between 9.37 and 9.38, but which is closer?

Answer: _____

Question 4

Round 0.66666666 to 3 decimal places. 0.666**6** is between 0.666 and 0.667, but which is closer?

Answer: _____

Question 5

Round £27.54667 to the nearest penny. £27.54**6** is between £27.54 and £27.55, but which is closer?

Answer: _____

Hint: Make sure you do chapter 1 place value and rounding before you do this chapter.

Remember: If the number in red is less than 5, round down, if the number in red is 5 or more, round up.

Hint: Drawing a number line can help you decide.

Remember: decimal places can be written as d.p.

Fill in the answers for questions 1 to 5. Draw number lines to help if you want to.

Hint: Rounding to the nearest penny is the same as rounding to 2 d.p.

1 Round off each of these numbers to the nearest whole number.

a 42.7 _____   b 51.9 _____   c 2.4 _____

d 3.5 _____   e 11.8 _____   f 15.1 _____

g 3.23 _____   h 81.22 _____   i 98.61 _____

j 66.53 _____   k 13.45 _____   l 8.99 _____

2 Put a circle around the correct answer. Each number must be rounded to 1 decimal place.

a 5.24   (5.2)   or   5.3   b 6.75   6.7   or   6.8   The first one has been done for you

c 8.88   8.8   or   8.9   d 14.53   14.5   or   14.6

e 11.621   11.6   or   11.7   f 58.452   58.4   or   58.5

g 8.554   8.5   or   8.6   h 3.751   3.7   or   3.8

3 Round off the following numbers to 2 decimal places.

a 4.657 _____   b 3.342 _____   c 8.875 _____

d 11.319 _____   e 32.897 _____   f 14.3246 _____

4 Complete the table, rounding each of the numbers to the given number of decimal places. All the answers are in the circle on the right, cross them off as you use them.

Question	Round to	Answer
6.235	1 d.p.	
5.54	1 d.p.	
8.493	2 d.p.	
6.244	2 d.p.	
7. 905	2 d.p.	
8.55	1 d.p.	
5.505	2 d.p.	
6.39	1 d.p.	
7.911	1 d.p.	
8.8821	3 d.p.	
7.896	2 d.p.	
5.48791	3 d.p.	

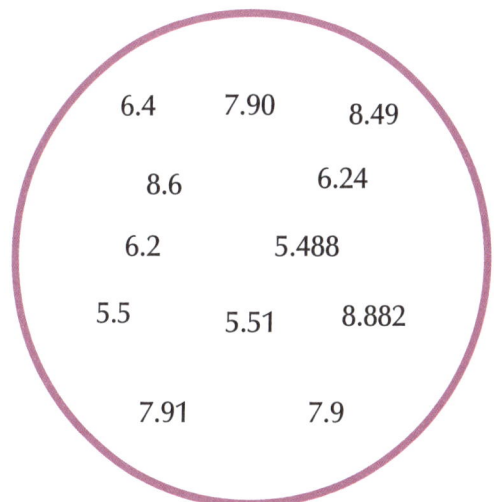

6.4   7.90   8.49
8.6   6.24
6.2   5.488
5.5   5.51   8.882
7.91   7.9

You need to know:

● How to express a ratio in its simplest form

EXAMPLE 1

Express the ratio 6 : 30 in its simplest form

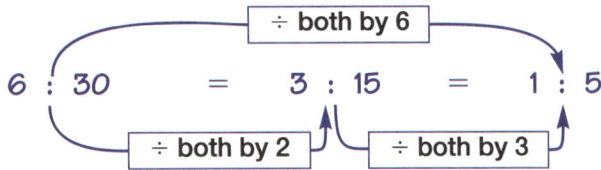

÷ both by 6

6 : 30   =   3 : 15   =   1 : 5

÷ both by 2   ÷ both by 3

Remember: When cancelling down a ratio, you can do it in one step (top version) or several steps (bottom version).

EXAMPLE 2

Express this ratio of quantities in its simplest form: 500 g : 2 kg

Step 1: There are 1000 g in a kg, so the ratio becomes 500 g : 2000 g
Step 2: Once the units are the same we won't need to write them down any more, so the ratio now is 500 : 2000
Step 3: Cancel down the ratio

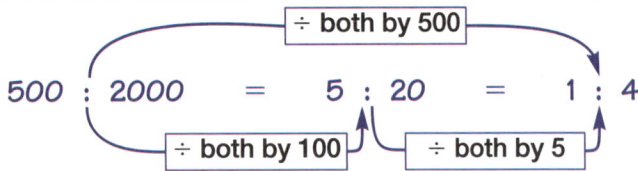

÷ both by 500

500 : 2000   =   5 : 20   =   1 : 4

÷ both by 100   ÷ both by 5

Warning: The answer to this is **not** 250 : 1

Hint: Before cancelling a ratio, the units must be the same.

EXAMPLE 3

Express 1.5 : 3.5 in its simplest form.

Step 1: Multiply both numbers by 10 to get rid of the decimal point so the ratio now is 15 : 35
Step 2: Cancel down by dividing both numbers by 5 so the ratio now is 3 : 7

Hint: When simplifying a decimal ratio, always multiply first to get rid of the decimal points.

Question 1

Express the following ratios in their simplest forms.

a 64 : 24 = 32 : 12 = _____ : _____ = _____ : _____

÷ by 2   ÷ by 2   ÷ by 2

b 2.5 : 3 = _____ : _____ = _____ : _____

× by 10   ÷ by 5

Follow the instructions and complete the cancelling down of the ratios in question 1.

Question 2

Express this ratio of quantities in its simplest form.

3 hours : 1 day = 3 : _____ = _____ : _____

Start question 2 by changing 1 day into 24 hours, then cancel down.

1   Express each of the following ratios in their simplest form.

    a   4 : 2 _____   **b**   6 : 2 _____

    c   9 : 3 _____   **d**   10 : 5 _____

    e   15 : 3 _____   **f**   16 : 4 _____

    g   20 : 5 _____   **h**   32 : 8 _____

Hint: These ratios all have an answer of something : 1

2   Express each of these ratios in their simplest form.

    a   6 : 8 _____   **b**   9 : 6 _____

    c   8 : 10   **d**   12 : 15 _____

    e   18 : 21   **f**   20 : 30 _____

    g   35 : 25   **h**   36 : 30 _____

Hint: These are slightly harder and don't have a 1 in the answer
e.g. 2 : 3 or 3 : 4

3   Circle the correct answer which shows the ratio in its simplest form.

    a   0.5 : 3   **Answer:**   1 : 4   or   1 : 5   or   1 : 6

    b   1.5 : 6   **Answer:**   1 : 3   or   1 : 4   or   1 : 5

    c   2 : 0.4   **Answer:**   5 : 1   or   4 : 1   or   2 : 1

    d   4.2 : 0.6   **Answer:**   8 : 1   or   7 : 1   or   6 : 1

Hint: Look at Example 3 on the help page.

4   Express the following ratio of quantities in their simplest form.

    a   6 kg : 20 kg   _____

    b   20 minutes : 1 hour   _____

    c   50p : £4   _____

    d   2 weeks : 6 days   _____

    e   30 cm : 6 m   _____

    f   500 ml : 2 litres   _____

    g   3 months : 2 years   _____

    h   2 days : 8 hours   _____

Remember: Make the units the same before cancelling.

You need to know:
- How to find the lines of symmetry of a shape ● How to find the order of rotation of a shape

EXAMPLE 1

Draw the lines of symmetry on the following shapes:

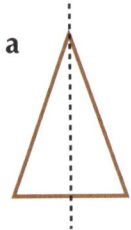

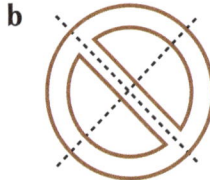

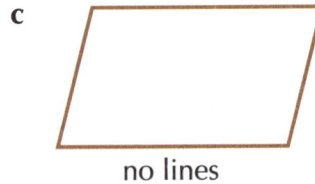

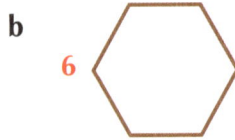

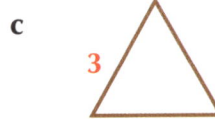

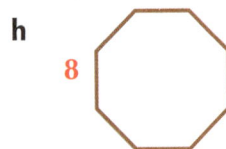

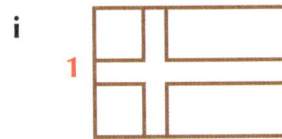

a   b   c

no lines

> **Remember:** A line of symmetry is a mirror line that cuts the shape exactly in half.

> **Hint:** Use a mirror to help you find the lines of symmetry.

EXAMPLE 2

What is the order of rotation of the shapes in Example 1?

a   order 1   b   order 2   c   order 2

> If a shape has no rotational symmetry, so it only fits onto itself once in one complete turn, it has order 1.

> **Remember:** The order of rotation is the number of times, in one complete turn, that a shape will fit onto itself.

Question 1

Draw the lines of symmetry on the following shapes.

a   4   b   6   c   3

d   4   e   1   f   4

g   2   h   8   i   1

> Draw the lines of symmetry on the shapes, the number in red tells you how many lines each shape should have.

Question 2

Write the letter of the above shapes in the correct columns below to describe the order of rotation of each shape.

Order 1	Order 2	Order 3	Order 4	Order 5	Order 6	Order 8
			a		b	

> Complete the table, the first two have been done for you.

1 Draw the lines of symmetry on the following shapes.

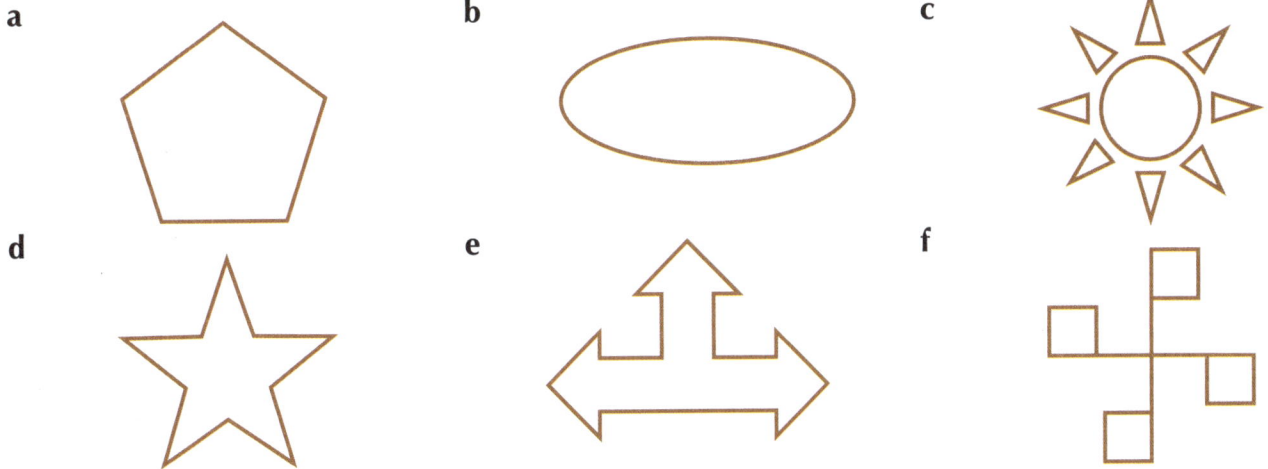

a

b

c

d

e

f

2 What is the order of rotation of the following shapes?

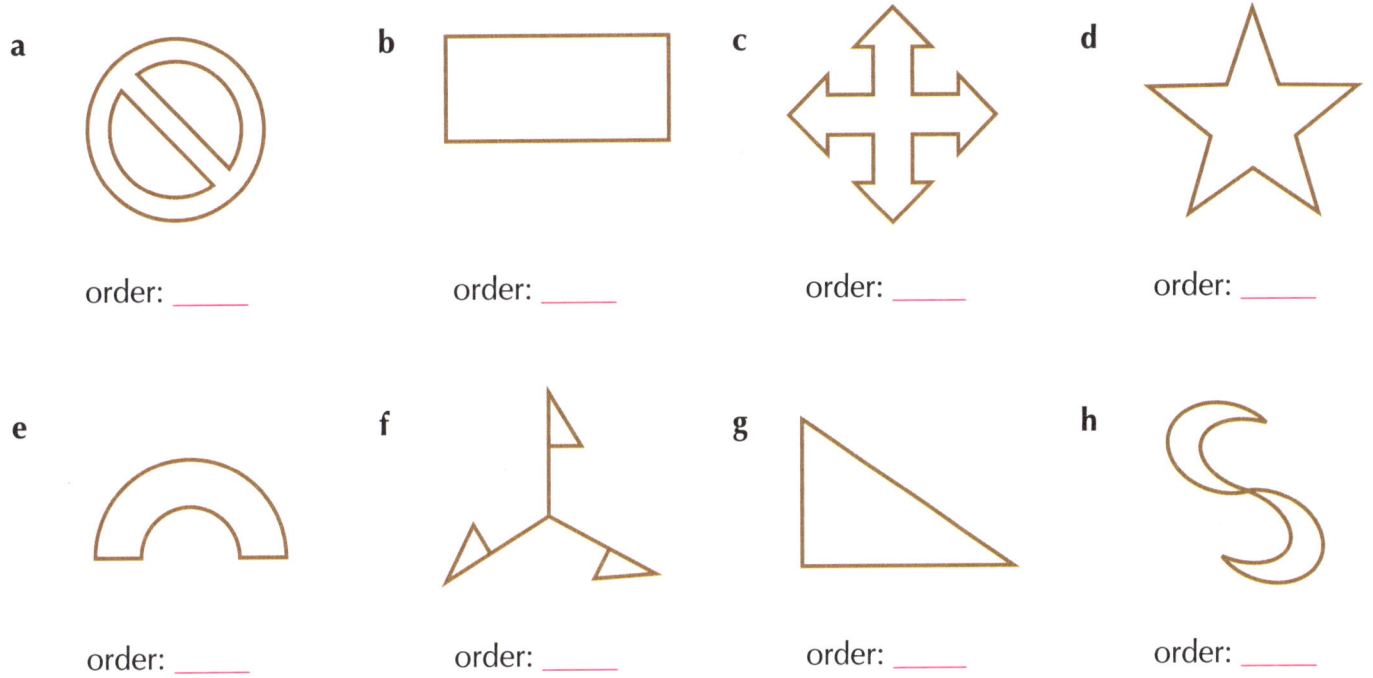

a

order: _____

b

order: _____

c

order: _____

d

order: _____

e

order: _____

f

order: _____

g

order: _____

h

order: _____

3 Complete the shapes on the grid so that the black line is a line of symmetry.

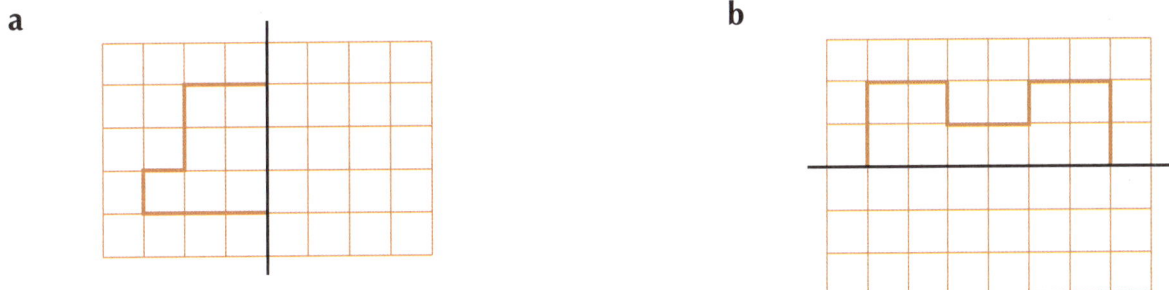

a

b

You need to know:
- How to find the mean, median, mode and range

EXAMPLE 1

The ages of the members of a netball club are as follows:

24, 16, 18, 30, 27, 21, 28, 21, 22

a What is the modal age?

Which age occurs the most?

mode = 21

b What is the median age?

First, arrange the ages in order of size.
16, 18, 21, 21, 22, 24, 27, 28, 30
The number in the middle of the list is 22

median = 22

c What is the mean age?

First, add all the ages together:
24 + 16 + 18 + 30 + 27 + 21 + 28 + 21 + 22 = 207

There are 9 members in the club:

207 ÷ 9 = 23

mean = 23

d What is the range in ages?

Highest - Lowest = 30 − 16 = 14

range = 14

EXAMPLE 2

Diane keeps a record of her scores (out of 10) for mental maths tests.
Her scores are as follows: 9, 7, 8, 9, 5, 6, 4, 9, 6, 8

a What is her median score?

First, arrange the scores in order of size: 4, 5, 6, 6, 7, 8, 8, 9, 9, 9
This time there are two numbers in the middle, so the median is
exactly half way between these two

median = $7\frac{1}{2}$

b What is her modal score?

Which score occurs the most often?

mode = 9

Remember: The mode is the number that occurs the most often.

Remember: The median is the middle value after the numbers have been put in order of size.

Remember: The mean is the sum of all the values divided by the total number of values.

Remember: The range is the highest value take away the lowest value.

Hint: To find the median when there are two middle numbers, simply add the two numbers together and divide by 2, e.g. 7 + 8 = 15
15 ÷ 2 = $7\frac{1}{2}$

Question 1

Keith keeps a record of the amount he spends each day for lunch during one week at work.

Day	Mon	Tues	Wed	Thurs	Fri
Amount	£3.15	£2.90	£3.15	£2.85	£2.65

a What is the mode of these amounts?   **mode = £2.90**

b What is the median of these amounts?
In order: £2.65, £2.85, _____, _____, _____   **median = £3.15**

c What is the mean of these amounts?
Total of amounts = £3.15 + £2.90 + _____ + _____ + £_____ = £14.70
mean = _____ ÷ 5 = _____   **mean = ____**

d What is the range of these amounts?
Highest – Lowest = _____ – _____ = _____   **range = ____**

Complete the workings to find out the answers to question 1.

1 The bar chart below shows the midday temperatures for one month in London.

Midday temperatures in London

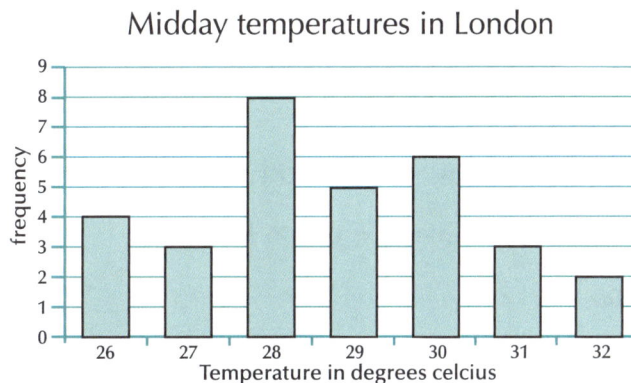

a On how many days was the midday temperature 26ºC? _____

b How many days were there in this month? _____

c What was the modal temperature during this month? _____

d What was the range in temperatures during this month? _____

Hint:
modal = most
often = tallest bar

2 A group of friends on a walking holiday walk the following distances each day:

14 miles, 20 miles, 10 miles, 13 miles, 11 miles, 10 miles

a What is the mean distance walked? _____

b What is the median distance walked? _____

c What is the modal distance walked? _____

d What is the range in distances walked? _____

3 The bar chart below shows the number of goals scored per match by a hockey team in 2004 and 2005.

Goals scored per match by hockey team

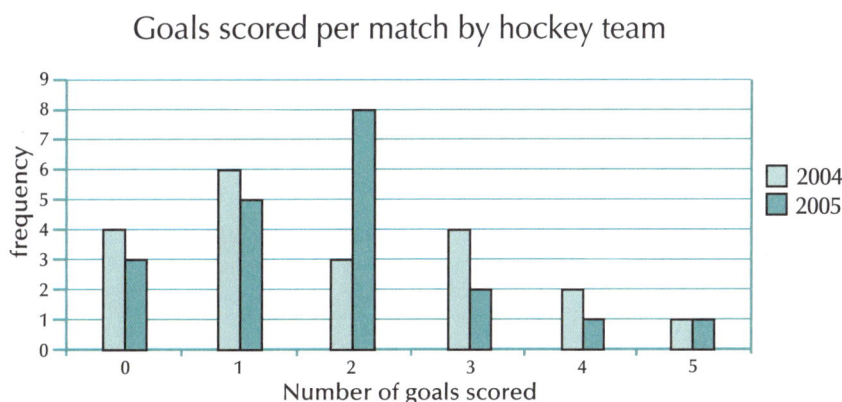

2004
2005

a What was the modal number of goals scored per match in 2004? _____

b What was the modal number of goals scored per match in 2005? _____

1 A formula for finding the approximate perimeter of a circle is:

perimeter = 6 × radius

What is the approximate perimeter of a circle with a radius of 3 cm? _____

2 The formula to work out the cost in Euros (€) of a taxi ride is:

C = 5 + 0.2 × km

How much does a 25 km taxi ride cost? _____

3 Give the next two numbers and a rule for these sequences.

a 5, 9, 13, 17, _____ , _____   **Rule:** _____

b 5, 10, 20, 40, _____ , _____   **Rule:** _____

c 10000, 1000, 100, 10, _____ , _____ **Rule:** _____

4 Complete the table:

	Question	Rounded off to	Answer
a	63.7	nearest whole number	
b	12.45	nearest whole number	
c	6.42	1 decimal place	
d	14.455	1 decimal place	
e	6.4933	2 decimal places	
f	1.11111	3 decimal places	
g	5.55555	3 decimal places	

5 Express each ratio in its simplest form.

a 6 : 3 _____   b 25 : 5 _____   c 4 : 16 _____

d 15 : 21 _____   e 25 : 20 _____   f 120 : 100 _____

g 1.5 : 2 _____   h 40p : £2 _____   i 3 kg : 250 g _____

6 Draw the lines of symmetry on the following shapes, and give the order of rotational symmetry of each one.

a

b
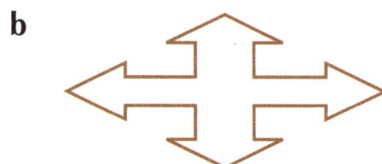

c
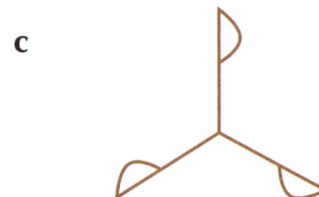

order: _____   order: _____   order: _____

7 Complete the shape on the grid so that the dotted black line is a line of symmetry.

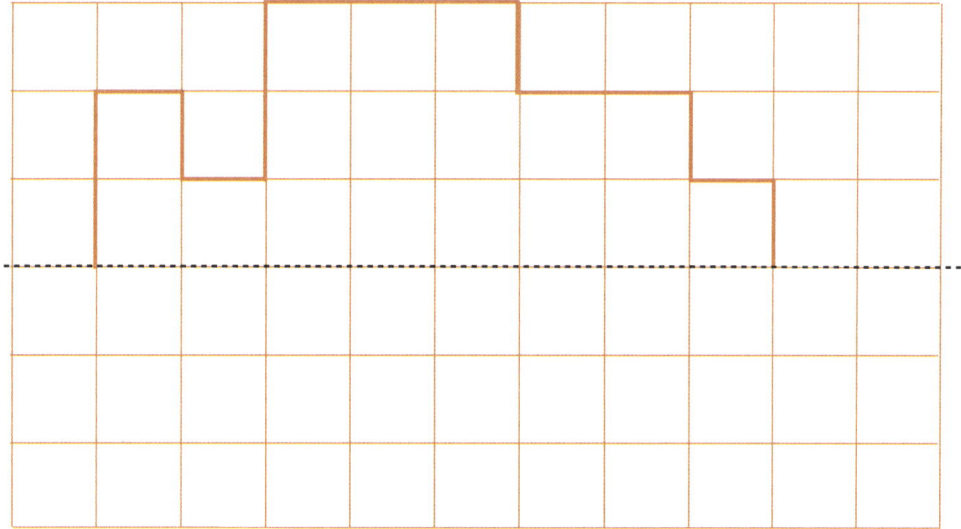

8 The bar chart below shows the midday temperatures for one month in Barcelona.

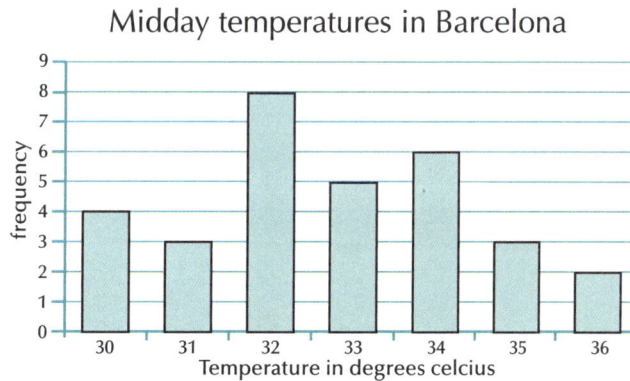

Midday temperatures in Barcelona

a On how many days was the midday temperature 30 °C? _____

b How many days were there in this month? _____

c What was the modal temperature during this month? _____

d What was the range in temperatures during this month? _____

9 Six friends go to 'Weight Checkers'. The amount of weight each friend lost is:

1.4 kg   2.0 kg   1.0 kg   1.3 kg   1.1 kg   1.0 kg

a What is the mean amount of weight lost? _____

b What is the median amount of weight lost? _____

c What is the modal amount of weight lost? _____

d What is the range in amount of weight lost? _____

You need to know:
- What a percentage is • How to convert between percentages, decimals and fractions

---

EXAMPLE 1

Write each percentage as a fraction in its lowest terms.

a 50% $50\% = \dfrac{50}{100} = \dfrac{50 \div 50}{100 \div 50}$ **Answer:** $\dfrac{1}{2}$ b 35% $35\% = \dfrac{35}{100} = \dfrac{35 \div 5}{100 \div 5}$ **Answer:** $\dfrac{7}{20}$

EXAMPLE 2

Write each percentage as a decimal.

a 75% $75\% = 75 \div 100$ **Answer:** 0.75   b 4% $4\% = 4 \div 100$ **Answer:** 0.04

EXAMPLE 3

Write each decimal as a percentage.

a 0.34 0.34×100 **Answer:** 34%   b 0.05 0.05×100 **Answer:** 5%

EXAMPLE 4

Write this fraction as a percentage and a decimal.

$\dfrac{3}{5}$ $\dfrac{3}{5} = \dfrac{3 \times 20}{5 \times 20} = \dfrac{60}{100} = 60\%$ **Answer:** 0.60 or 0.6

EXAMPLE 5

Write each decimal as a fraction.

a 0.4 $0.4 = \dfrac{4}{10} = \dfrac{4 \div 2}{10 \div 2}$ **Answer:** $\dfrac{2}{5}$ b 0.11 $0.11 = \dfrac{11}{100}$ **Answer:** $\dfrac{11}{100}$ cannot cancel down any further

Question 1

Complete the workings to do the following conversions.

a 25% to a fraction $25\% = \dfrac{\quad}{100} = \dfrac{25 \div}{100 \div} = \dfrac{1}{\quad}$

b 10% to a decimal $10\% = \dfrac{\quad}{} \div 100 = \dfrac{\quad}{}$

c 0.6 to a fraction $0.6 = \dfrac{\quad}{10} = \dfrac{6 \div}{10 \div} = \dfrac{\quad}{5}$

d $\dfrac{3}{50}$ to a percentage $\dfrac{3}{50} = \dfrac{3 \times}{50 \times} = \dfrac{\quad}{100} = \underline{\quad}\%$

e 0.056 to a percentage $0.056 \times \underline{\quad} = \underline{\quad}\%$

f $\dfrac{3}{4}$ to a decimal $\dfrac{3}{4} = \dfrac{3 \times}{4 \times} = \dfrac{\quad}{100} = \underline{\quad}\% = 0.\underline{\quad}$

Remember: 'per cent' means 'out of 100', so any percentage can be written as a fraction whose denominator is 100.

Hint: When cancelling down fractions divide the top and bottom by the biggest number you can find that will go into both.

Remember: When dividing by 100, move the decimal point two places to the left. When multiplying by 100, move the decimal point two places to the right.

Remember: After the decimal point comes the tenths column, so $0.4 = \dfrac{4}{10}$ then comes the hundreths column, so $0.11 = \dfrac{11}{100}$

Complete the workings to find the answers for question 1.

1 Complete the table.

Percentage	Decimal	Fraction	Workings
25%	0.25	$\frac{1}{4}$	$25 \div 100 = 0.25 \quad \frac{25}{100} = \frac{1}{4}$
50%			
	0.75		
		$\frac{1}{10}$	
	0.4		
70%			
	0.2		
		$\frac{3}{5}$	
	0.45		
15%			
	0.17		
		$\frac{7}{25}$	

2 Sally saves 65% of her pocket money each week. What percentage does she spend?

_____

3 Put the following numbers in order of size starting with the smallest.

8% $\frac{3}{10}$ 0.63 $\frac{4}{5}$ 0.35   70% _____

> Change the decimals and fractions to percentages, then compare them

4 What percentage of the following shapes are **unshaded**?

a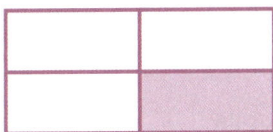

b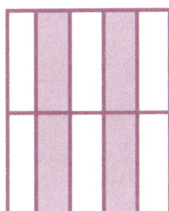

c

d

You need to know:

● How to find a percentage of an amount with and without a calculator

---

EXAMPLE 1

Without a calculator find the following:

a 10% of £40   **b** 10% of $500   **c** 10% of 6 m

a 10% of £40 = 40 ÷ 10   **Answer:** £4

b 10% of $500 = 500 ÷ 10   **Answer:** $50

c 10% of 6 m = 6 ÷ 10   **Answer:** 0.6 m

> **Remember:**
> To find 10% of a number, divide the number by 10 – if the number ends in a 0, just cross the zero off.

EXAMPLE 2

Without a calculator find the following:

a 20% of £60   **b** 30% of €200   **c** 80% of 12 m

a 20% of £60: 10% = 60 ÷ 10 = 6   20% = 6 × 2   **Answer:** £12

b 30% of €200: 10% = 200 ÷ 10 = 20   30% = 20 × 3   **Answer:** €60

c 80% of 12 m: 10% = 12 ÷ 10 = 1.2   80% = 1.2 × 8   **Answer:** 9.6 m

> **Hint:** Always find 10% first, then × by 2 for 20%, 3 for 30%, 4 for 40% etc.

EXAMPLE 3

Use a calculator to find the following:

a 5% of £300   **b** 12% of 80 kg   **c** 85% of 12 litres

a 5% of £300: (5 ÷ 100) × 300   **Answer:** £15

b 12% of 80 Kg: (12 ÷ 100) × 80   **Answer:** 9.6 kg

c 85% of 12 litres: (85 ÷ 100) × 12   **Answer:** 10.2 litres

> **Remember:**
> $18\% = 18 \div 100$, so 18% (or $\frac{18}{100}$) of something
> $= 18 \div 100 \times$ something

Question 1

Without using a calculator, work out the percentages on the left, and join them with a line to their correct answer on the right.

10% of £500	£45
10% of £7	£50
20% of £70	£54
30% of £150	£28
70% of £40	£14
90% of £60	£0.70

> Complete question 1, one of them has been done for you.

Question 2

A school has 1600 pupils. 12% of the pupils go home for lunch. 32% of the pupils bring sandwiches, and the rest have school dinners. How many pupils do each of these?

home: 12% of 1600 = (12 ÷ _____) × 1600 = _____ pupils

sandwiches: 32% of 1600 = (_____ ÷ _____) × 1600 = _____ pupils

dinners: 1600 − _____ − _____ = _____ pupils

> Complete the workings for question 2

> **Hint:** To calculate 'dinners':
> 1600 − home − sandwiches = ?

1 Without a calculator, find:

   a 10 % of 70 kg = _____   **b** 10% of £300 = _____

   c 10% of 4 km = _____   **d** 10% of £8 = _____

2 Without a calculator, work out the following percentages, then circle the correct answer.

   a 20% of $400 = $4 $8 $40 $80

   b 30% of 50 m =   5 m   10 m   15 m   20 m

   c 70% of £12 =   £84   £8.40   £1.20   £0.12

   d 15% of 60 cm =   3 cm   6 cm   9 cm   12 cm

You can use a calculator for the following questions.

3 Mr Williams earns £12 000. He receives a pay rise of 4%. How much is this?

   _____

4 At a company employing 860 people, 65% are women. How many women are there?

   _____

5 A advertisement for a jar of coffee states that a 'special offer' jar has 25% extra free.
   The usual weight of the jar is 200 g. How much extra is there in the 'special offer' jar?

   _____

6 An estate agent charges 1.5% commission on every house she sells.
   How much would she earn on a house that she sells for £96 000?

   _____

7 VAT (Value Added Tax) is added to the price of goods sold in the shops. VAT is 17.5% of the cost of the
   item. What is the VAT which is added to:

   a A microwave oven costing £85 (give your answer to the nearest penny)?

   _____

   b A stereo costing £192?

   _____

   c A computer costing £686?

   Remember: When
   dealing with £ and
   pence there must only
   be two numbers after
   the decimal point.

   _____

You need to know:
- How to use number machines ● How to solve simple equations

EXAMPLE 1

Use the function machine below to complete the table.

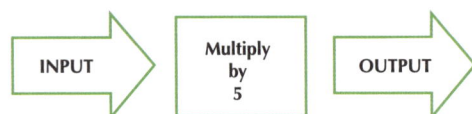

INPUT ➤ ADD 6 ➤ OUTPUT

Answers:
$3 + 6 = 9$
$7 + 6 = 13$
$18 - 6 = 12$
$25 - 6 = 19$

INPUT	OUTPUT
3	9
7	13
12	18
19	25

Remember: The input is the number which goes into the function machine, and the output is the number which comes out

Hint: If you know the output and want to find the input, reverse the machine (do the opposite)

EXAMPLE 2

Solve these equations:

a $a + 6 = 10$ $a = 10 - 6$ **Answer:** $a = 4$
b $b - 4 = 12$ $b = 12 + 4$ **Answer:** $b = 16$
c $3c = 15$ $c = 15 \div 3$ **Answer:** $c = 5$
d $\frac{d}{10} = 4$ $d = 4 \times 10$ **Answer:** $d = 40$

Remember: When solving an equation, 'do the opposite':
opposite of + is –
opposite of – is +
opposite of × is ÷
opposite of ÷ is ×

Question 1

Use the function machine to complete the table.

INPUT ➤ Multiply by 5 ➤ OUTPUT

INPUT	OUTPUT
3	3 x 5 =
5	5 x 5 = 25
9	9 x 5 = 45
7	35
50 ÷ 5 =	50
	100

Complete the table

Question 2

Solve these equations.

a $x + 11 = 15$ $x = 15 - \underline{\quad} = \underline{\quad}$
b $y - 5 = 9$ $y = 9 + \underline{\quad} = \underline{\quad}$
c $7w = 42$ $w = 42 \div \underline{\quad} = \underline{\quad}$
d $\frac{z}{5} = 8$ $z = 8 \times \underline{\quad} = \underline{\quad}$
e $12 + v = 18$ $v = 18 - \underline{\quad} = \underline{\quad}$
f $4 = y - 1$ $y = 4 + \underline{\quad} = \underline{\quad}$

Complete the workings for question 2

1 Use the function machines to complete the tables.

a

INPUT → SUBTRACT 8 → OUTPUT

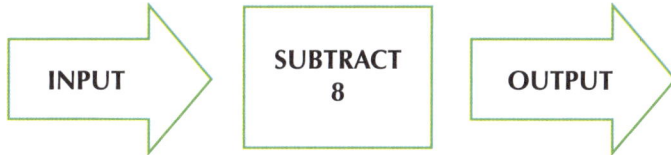

INPUT	OUTPUT
10	
12	
	6
	12

b

INPUT → DIVIDE BY 3 → OUTPUT

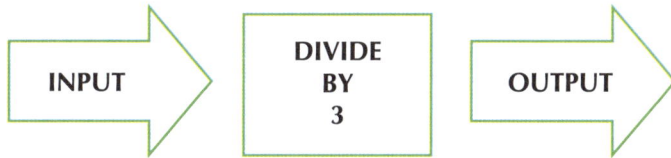

INPUT	OUTPUT
9	
12	
	7
	12

c

INPUT → ADD 25 → OUTPUT

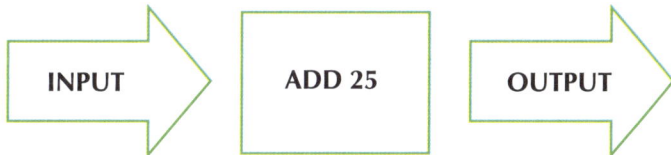

INPUT	OUTPUT
4	
14	
	49
	106

2 Solve the following equations, then join the equation on the left to the correct answer on the right.

Equation	Working	Answer
$x + 4 = 10$	$x = 10 - 4 = 6$	$x = 10$
$x - 6 = 13$		$x = 50$
$6x = 60$		$x = 19$
$\frac{x}{3} = 4$		$x = 9$
$2x = 30$		$x = 6$
$x + 11 = 20$		$x = 20$
$\frac{x}{5} = 4$		$x = 15$
$x - 25 = 25$		$x = 12$

The first equation has been done for you.

3 Tick the equations below which give an answer of $y = 5$. Put a cross next to the ones that don't.

$y + 5 = 10$ ✓ ($y = 10 - 5 = 5$) $3y = 15$ _____ $\frac{y}{2} = 10$ _____

$y - 10 = 5$ _____ $y + 12 = 18$ _____ $y - 1 = 4$ _____

The first one has been done for you.

You need to know:

● How to read and understand a conversion graph

EXAMPLE 1

This is a graph showing the conversion between kilograms (kg) and pounds (lb).

Conversion graph for kg and lb

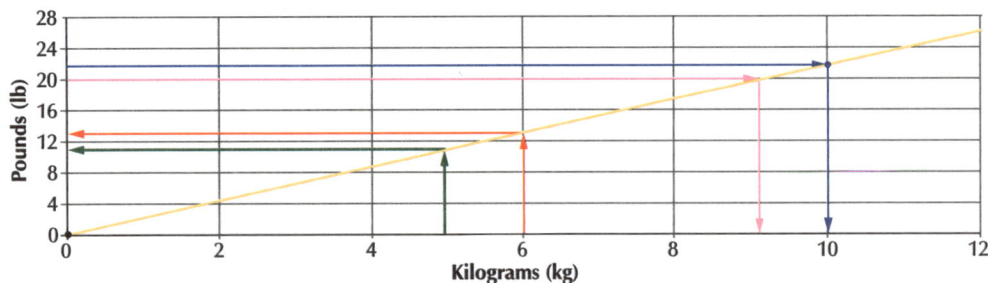

Use the graph to convert:

a   6 kg to Pounds (lb)
b   5 kg to Pounds (lb)
c   20 lb to kg
d   22 lb to kg
e   Roughly how many pounds are equivalent to 1 kg?   2.2 lb

(a) red line from 6 kg = 13 lb
(b) green line from 5 kg = 11 lb
(c) pink line from 20lb = 9 kg
(d) blue line from 22lb = 10 kg

Hint: When using a conversion graph, do not be afraid to draw on it to help you answer the questions.

In Example 1, the lines have been drawn for you to show how to answer the questions.

Part e:
Look at 10 kg
   10 kg = 22 lb
÷ both numbers by 10 to give
   1 kg = 2.2 lb

Question 1

The following graph shows the approximate conversion of Euros (€) to British pounds (£) during spring 2005.

Conversion graph for Euros and Pounds

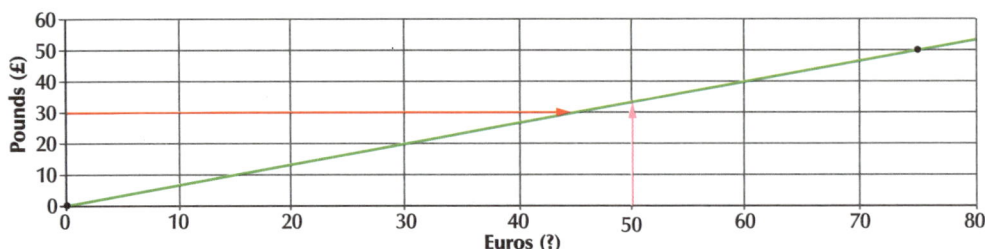

Use the graph to convert:

a   £30 to euros (€)   _____
b   £10 to euros (€)   _____
c   50€ to pounds (£)   _____
d   25€ to pounds (£)   _____
e   Approximately how many euros are equivalent to £1?   _____

Draw your own lines for question 1 on the graph - use different colours so you don't get in a muddle, **a** and **c** have been started for you.

Hint: Part **e**, find how many euros are worth £10, then divide by 10.

1 A family plan a trip to America. The graph below shows the conversion between British pounds (£) and American dollars ($).

Conversion graph for Pounds to Dollars

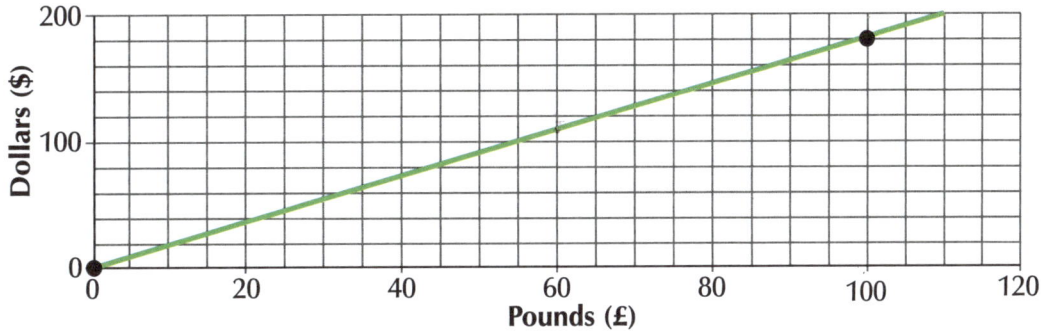

Use the graph to approximately convert:

a £60 to dollars   £60 = $ _____   **b** £45 to dollars   £45 = $ _____

c $200 to pounds $200 = £ _____   **d** $90 to pounds $90 = £ _____

2 A washing machine repair firm use the following graph to work out the cost to repair a machine. The cost depends on the number of hours it takes.

Cost of repairing a washing machine

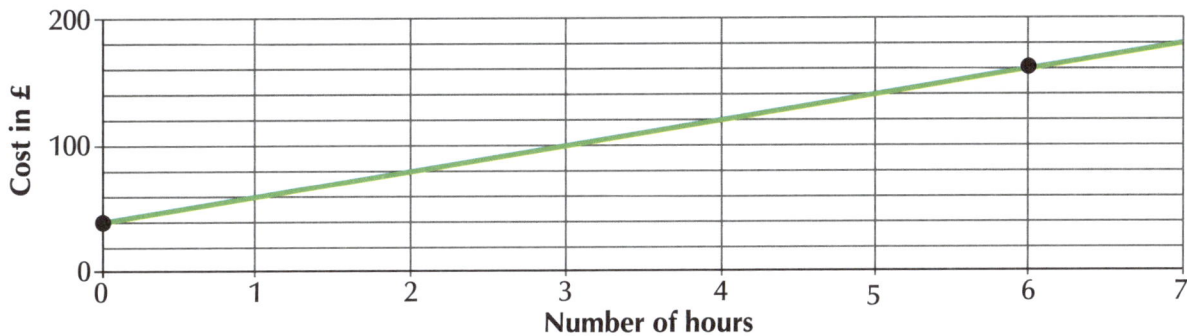

Use the graph to find the cost of repairing a machine if it takes:

a 4 hours   Cost for 4 hours = £ _____   **b** $2\frac{1}{2}$ hours   Cost for $2\frac{1}{2}$ hours = £ _____

c Mr Davies was charged £70 to repair his machine. How long did it take? _____

You need to know:
- How to plot coordinates in the first quadrant ● The names of common 2-D and 3-D shapes

Question 1

Join, with a line, the shapes to their names:

2-D

triangle

square

rectangle

kite

rhombus

parallelogram

trapezium

pentagon

hexagon

octagon

3-D

cube

cuboid

square based
pyramid

triangular based
pyramid

triangular prism

cylinder

sphere

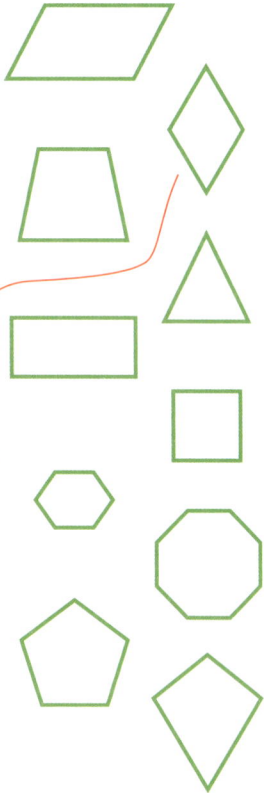

> Complete question 1, four of the shapes have already been done for you.

Question 2

Are the following sets of lines parallel, perpendicular, or neither?

a   **b**   **c**   **d**   **e**   **f**

parallel   neither   perpendicular   _____   _____   _____

> Complete question 2. Add the ≥ symbol to the parallel lines and the ⌐ symbol to the perpendicular ones. **a**, **b** and **c** have been done for you.

> **Remember:** Parallel lines are lines that never meet. Perpendicular lines are lines that meet at 90°.

Question 3

Look at the grid on the right.

a Write down the coordinates of the points A, B and C.
A (1,1)   B (5,___)   C(___,___)

b Plot the point D so that ABCD is a parallelogram. What are the coordinates of D?   D (___,___)

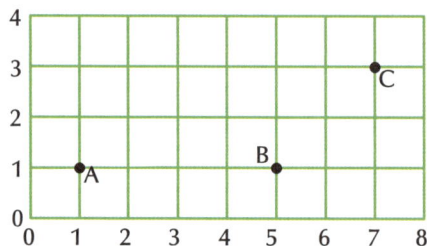

> **Remember:** When writing coordinates, it is the number across first → then the number up ↑

> Complete question 3 parts **a** and **b**. Plot the point D on the grid.

1 What 2-D shapes are being described below?

a I have 4 sides, they are all the same length. All my angles are 90°. _____

b I have 5 sides. _____

c I have 4 sides, two of them are parallel, the other two are not parallel. _____

d I only have 3 sides. _____

e I have 4 sides, two of them are parallel to each other, and the other two are parallel to each other. None of my angles are 90°. _____

2 What 3-D shapes are being described below?

a I have 6 faces, they are all the same size and shape. _____

b Two of my faces are circles, the other is a rectangle. _____

c I have 5 vertices (corners) and 4 of my faces are triangles. _____

d I have no vertices. _____

e I have 5 faces and 6 vertices. Two of my faces are triangles and 3 are rectangles. _____

3 Plot each of these points on the grid below. Join them in alphabetical order, and describe the shape you have made.

A(3,1) B(6,1) C(8,3) D(8,6) E(6,8) F(3,8) G(1,6) H(1,3) I(3,1) _____

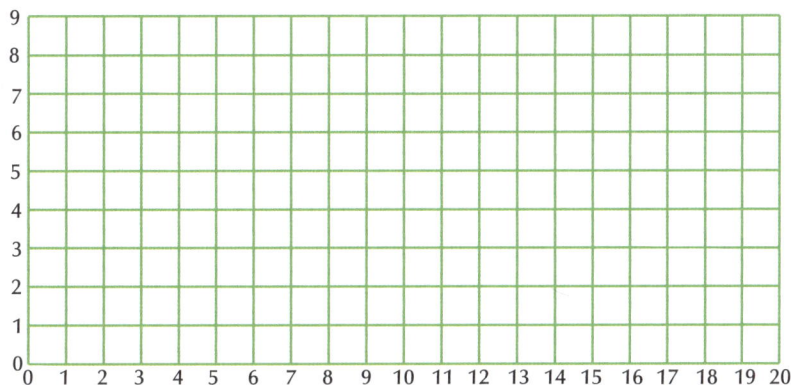

4 Plot each of these points on the grid above. Join them in alphabetical order, and describe the shape you have made.

A(10,4) B(15,4) C(15,3) D(18,5) E(15,7) F(15,6) G(10,6) H(10,4) _____

1 Complete the table below.

Percentage	Decimal	Fraction
	0.5	
75%		
		$\frac{3}{10}$
	0.35	
5%		
		$\frac{13}{20}$

2 Put the following in order of size, smallest first.

17% $\frac{2}{10}$ 0.26 $\frac{1}{4}$ 99%

_____

3 What percentage of each shape is shaded?

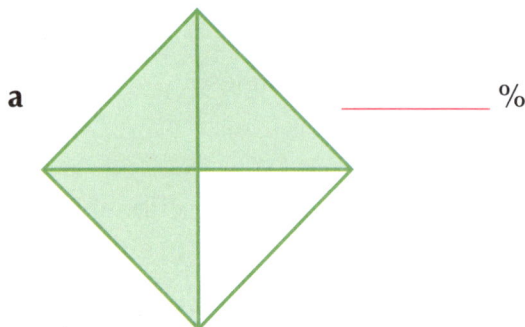

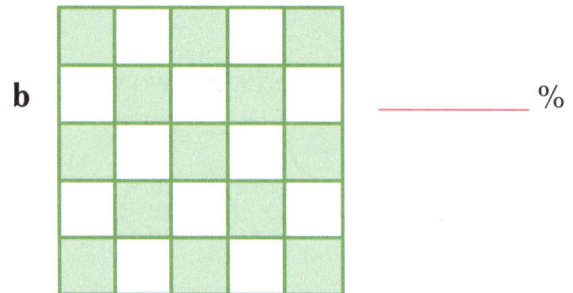

a   _____ %

b   _____ %

4 Find:

a 10% of 60 kg = _____

b 10% of £5 = _____

c 20% of 8 km = _____

d 15% of 40 km = _____

5 A garage door costs £450 + VAT. Find the VAT (17.5%) that will be added.

_____

6 Use the function machine to complete the table.

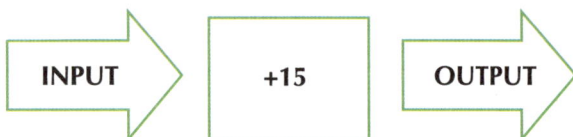

INPUT ⟹ +15 ⟹ OUTPUT

Input	Output
12	
	58

7 Solve each of the following equations:

a x + 8 = 14

x = _____

b x − 3 = 10

x = _____

c 4x = 20

x = _____

d 6 × a = 18

a = _____

e $\frac{a}{3}$ = 9

a = _____

f a ÷ 10 = 20

a = _____

8 We can use the conversion graph below to convert between £'s and €'s.

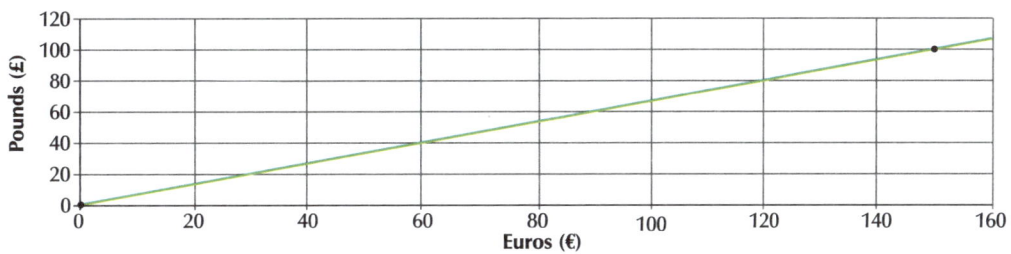

Conversion graph for Euros and Pounds

Use the graph to approximately convert:

a £60 to euros   £60 = _____ €

b 60€ to pounds   60€ = £_____

9 What shapes are being described?

a I have 4 sides which are not all the same length. My opposite sides are the same length, and all my angles are 90°.

_____

b I have 8 sides.

_____

c I have 5 faces, 4 of them are triangles, and the other is a square.

_____

d I have 4 sides which are all the same length. I do not have a 90° angle.

_____

10 Plot each of these points on the grid.

A(1,4) B(0,2) C(2,2) D(1,4) E(4,5) F(5,3) G(2,2)

Join them in alphabetical order.

What shape have you drawn?

_____

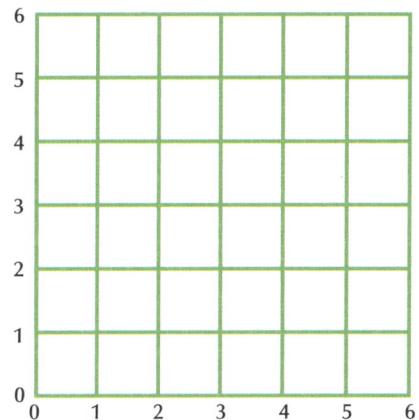

You need to know:
- How to measure angles using a protractor
- How to calculate angles using 'angles on a straight line' and 'angles at a point'

EXAMPLE 1

Use the drawn protractor to measure the angles shown. What type of angles are they?

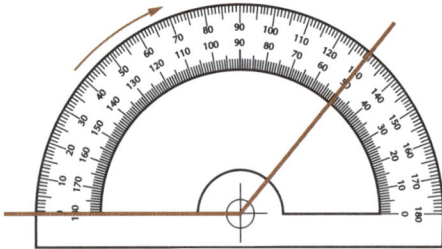

Answer: 130° Obtuse

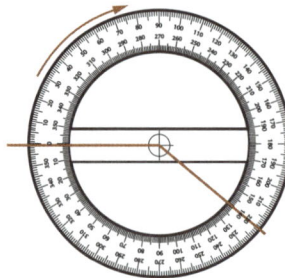

Answer: 220° Reflex

> **Remember:** Read the scale which starts at 0, in both **a** and **b** it is the outside scale, and reading clockwise.

> **Remember:** The different types of angles are:
> acute = 0° to 90°
> obtuse = 90° to 180°
> reflex = 180° to 360°.

Question 1

Use the drawn protractor to measure the angles shown. What type of angles are they?

a

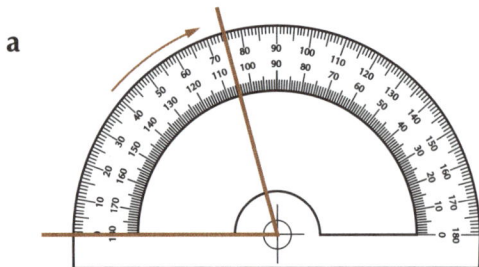

Answer: _____

b

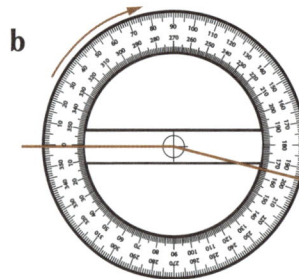

Answer: _____

> Measure these angles and write the answers in the spaces provided.

EXAMPLE 2

Calculate the size of the angles marked with a letter.

a 150° ⟋ a $a = 180 - 150$ Answer: 30°

b 300° ⟋ b $b = 360 - 300$ Answer: 60°

c ⟋ 55 $c = 90 - 55$ Answer: 45°

> **Remember:** Angles on a straight line add up to 180°.

> **Remember:** Angles around a point add up to 360°.

Question 2

Calculate the size of the angles marked with a letter:

a 20° ⟋ d $d = \underline{\quad} - 20 = \underline{\quad}°$

b e ⌐ $e = 360 - \underline{\quad} - \underline{\quad} = \underline{\quad}°$
   ⟋ 120°

> **Remember:**
> ⌐ means 90°.

> Complete the calculations and answers for question 2.

1 Use a protractor to find the size of each marked angle. What type of angles are they?

a

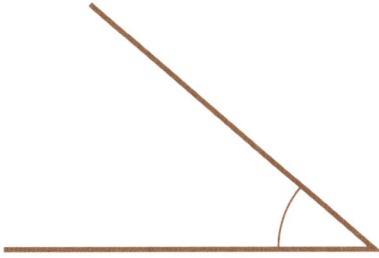

size: _____   type: _____

b

size: _____   type: _____

2 Use a protractor to draw the following angles:

a 115°

b 270°

Remember: Show all your workings

3 Calculate the size of the angles marked with a letter:

a

135° a

a = _____

b

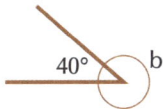
40° b

b = _____

c

63°
c

c = _____

d

120°
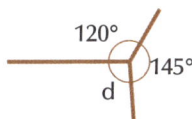
145°
d

d = _____

e

72°
e

e = _____

f

f

86°

f = _____

You need to know:
- How to draw a circle ● What the radius, diameter, and circumference of a circle arc

EXAMPLE 1

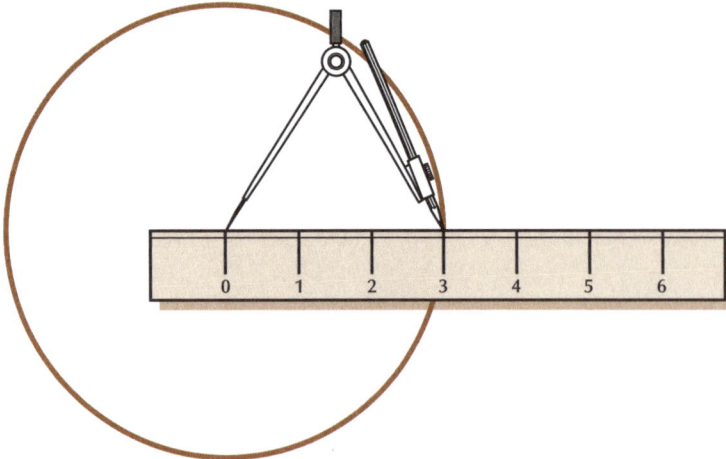

a What is the radius of this circle?   **Answer:** 3 cm
b What is the diameter of this circle?

diameter = 2 × radius = 2 × 3 = 6   **Answer:** 6 cm

Remember: The radius of a circle is the distance from the centre to the edge.

Remember: The diameter of a circle is the distance right across the circle going through the centre
diameter = 2 × radius

Hint: Always use compasses to draw a circle, and be as accurate as you can.

EXAMPLE 2

Draw a circle with a diameter of 4 cm

Step 1: Find the radius:
radius = $\frac{1}{2}$ of diameter
radius = $\frac{1}{2}$ of 4 = 2 cm
Step 2: Open your compasses to 2 cm (use a ruler)
Step 3: Draw a dot for the centre of your circle, put you compass point on the dot and draw the circle

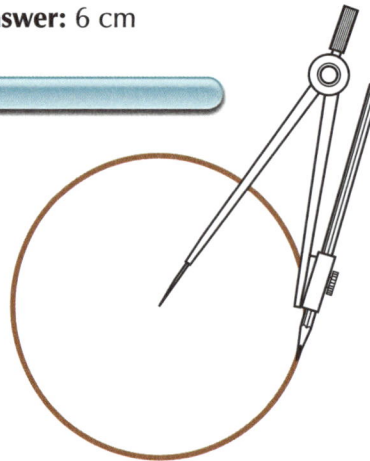

Question 1

Accurately draw a semicircle with diameter 5cm.
radius = $\frac{1}{2}$ of diameter
radius = $\frac{1}{2}$ of _____ = _____ cm

Calculate the radius of the semicircle, then use your compasses and the line given to draw the semicircle.

Question 2

On the circles drawn below, draw or show the following:

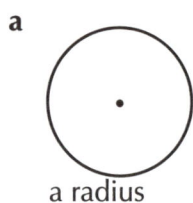

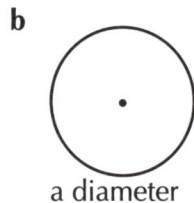

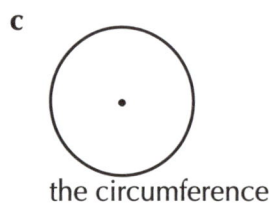

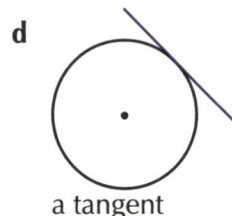

a   **b**   **c**   **d**

a radius   a diameter   the circumference   a tangent

Draw the answers onto the circles, **d** has been done for you; a tangent is a straight line that touches the circle.

1 Measure the radius of this circle.

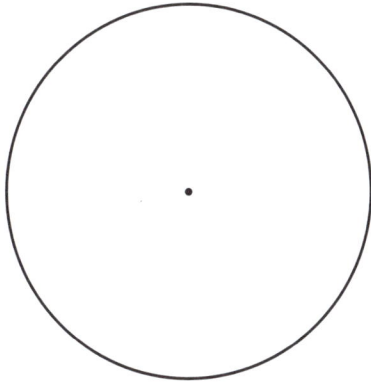

2 Measure the diameter of this circle.

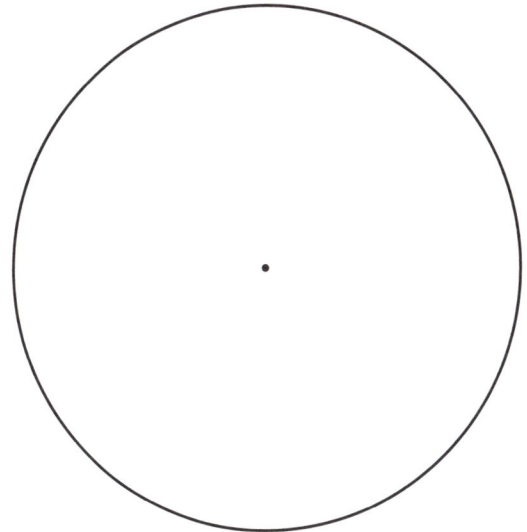

Hint: Make sure you give your answers using the units shown

radius = _____ mm

3 Draw a circle with a radius of 4 cm. Use the dot below as the centre.

diameter = _____ cm

4 Accurately draw this $\frac{1}{4}$ circle below.

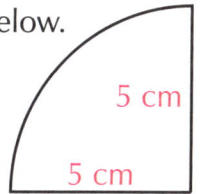

5 cm

5 cm

_____

5 What is the radius of a circle which has a diameter of 9 cm? _____

6 What is the diameter of a circle with a radius of 42 mm? _____

7 Accurately draw the following shape:

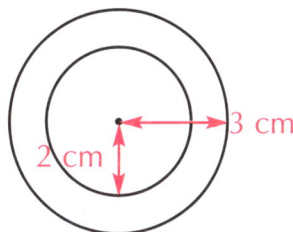

3 cm

2 cm

You need to know:
- How to use scales in scale drawings ● How to draw and recognise nets of shapes

EXAMPLE 1

This is a scale drawing of a piece of wood

The scale is 1 cm : 1 m

How long is this piece of wood in real life?

Answer: The drawing is 5 cm long.

Every 1 cm on the drawing is worth 1 m in real life, so the wood is _5 m_ long.

> **Remember:** Measure the scale drawing accurately with a ruler.

EXAMPLE 2

The section of road shown below is on a map with a scale of 1 : 200 000.

A321

How long is the A321 section in real life?

Answer: The road measures 3 cm long on the map.

3 cm on the map = 3 × 200 000 = 600 000 cm on the ground
600 000 ÷ 100 = 6000 m   6000 ÷ 1000 = 6 km

> **Hint:** The scale of 1 : 200 000 means that every 1cm on the map is worth 200 000 cm on the ground.

> **Remember:** 100 cm = 1 m 1000 m = 1 km

Question 1

This is a scale drawing of a field. The scale is 1 cm : 200 m

In real life this field is 200 m wide and _____ m long.

> Find the length of the field to complete the sentence; the width has been done for you.

Question 2

This is the scale drawing of a square tile. The scale is 1 : 10

How wide is this tile in real life?
Answer: _____ cm

> Measure the tile on the scale drawing then calculate its length in real life.

Question 3

Imagine this cube folded out flat.
Put a tick underneath the correct nets for this cube.

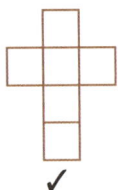

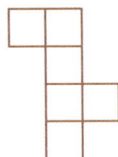

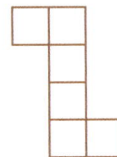

> **Remember:** A net is a flat diagram of a 3-D shape.

✓   ✗

> Tick the three correct nets and put a cross under the wrong ones. The first two have been done for you.

1 Look at the plan of this garden.
The scale is 1 cm to 2 m. In real life:

a What is the length of the garden?

_____

b What is the length of the path?

_____

c What is the radius of the pond?

_____

length of garden

Pond

length
of
path

Path

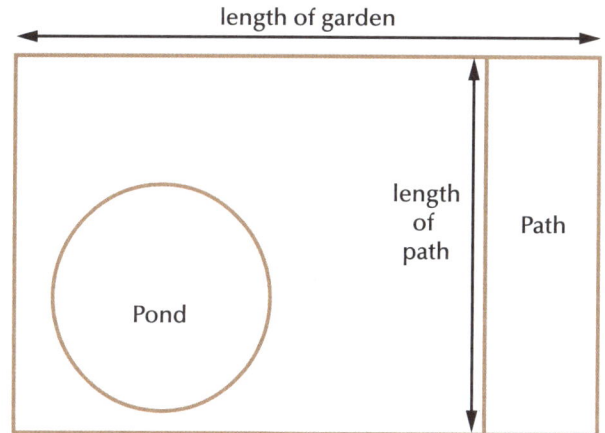

Remember: The radius of a circle is the
distance from the centre to the edge

2 The map below is drawn to a scale of 1 : 300 000.

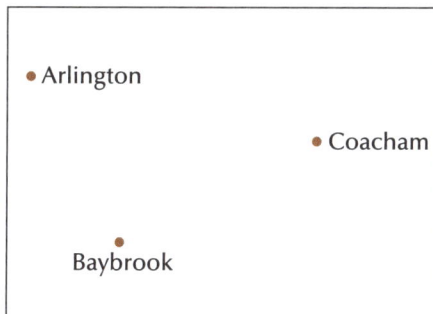

• Arlington

• Coacham

•
Baybrook

What is the direct distance in kilometres:

a from Arlington to Coacham?

_____

b from Baybrook to Coacham?

_____

3 Draw on the grid below an accurate net for this cuboid:

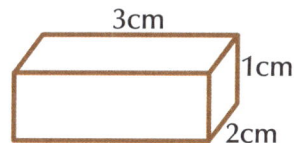

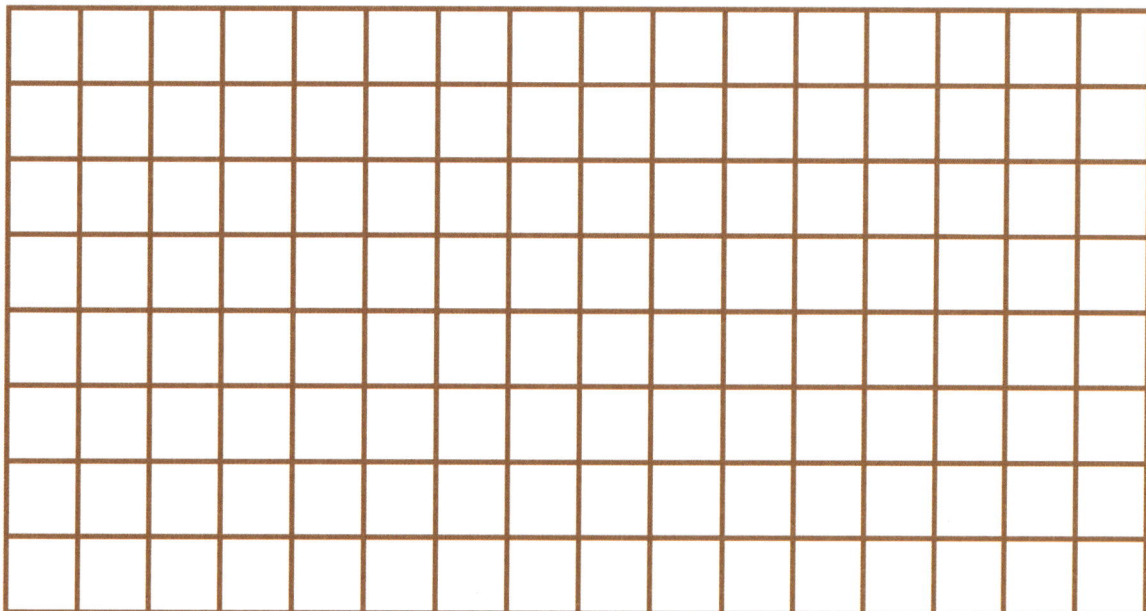

3cm

1cm

2cm

1 Use a protractor to find the size of the following angles. What type of angles are they?

a

size: _____ type: _____

b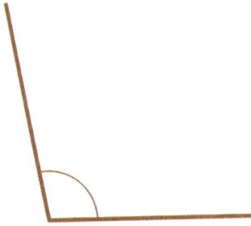

size: _____ type: _____

c

size: _____ type: _____

2 Calculate the size of the angles marked with a letter.

a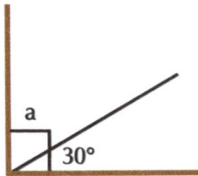

a = _____

b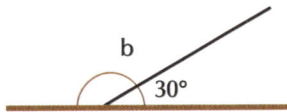

b = _____

c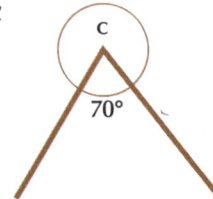

c = _____

d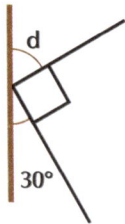

d = _____

e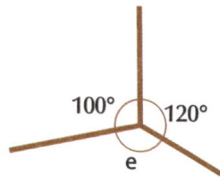

e = _____

f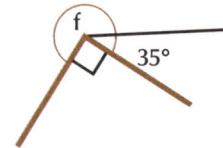

f = _____

3 **a** Measure the radius of this circle.

radius= _____

b Measure the diameter of this circle.

diameter= _____

4 What is the radius of a circle that has a diameter of 10 m? _____

5 Accurately draw this shape.

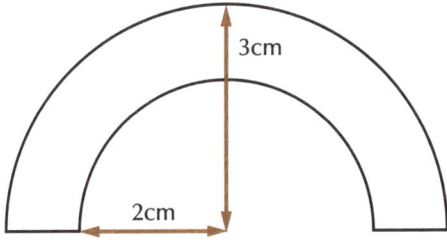

3cm

2cm

6 Here is a scale drawing of a new patio.
It has been drawn to a scale of 1 cm : 2 m.

In real life:

a How long is the patio? _____

b How long is a bench? _____

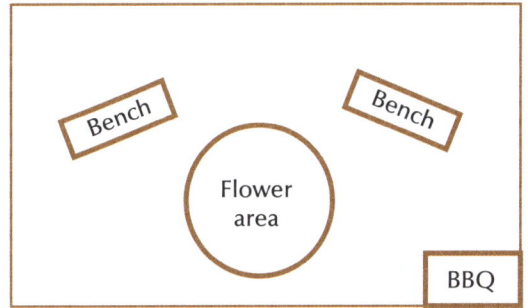

Bench

Bench

Flower
area

BBQ

7 The map below is drawn to a scale of 1 : 200 000.

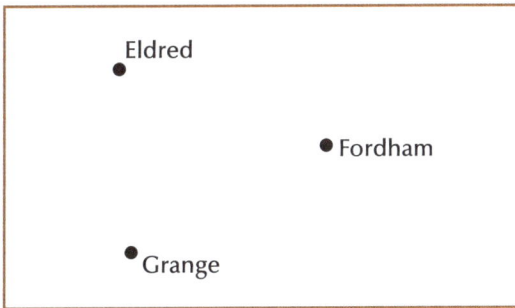

Eldred

Fordham

Grange

What is the direct distance in kilometres:

a from Eldred to Grange?

_____

b from Fordham to Grange?

_____

8 Draw an accurate net for this cuboid on the grid below.

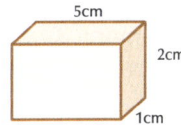

5cm

2cm

1cm

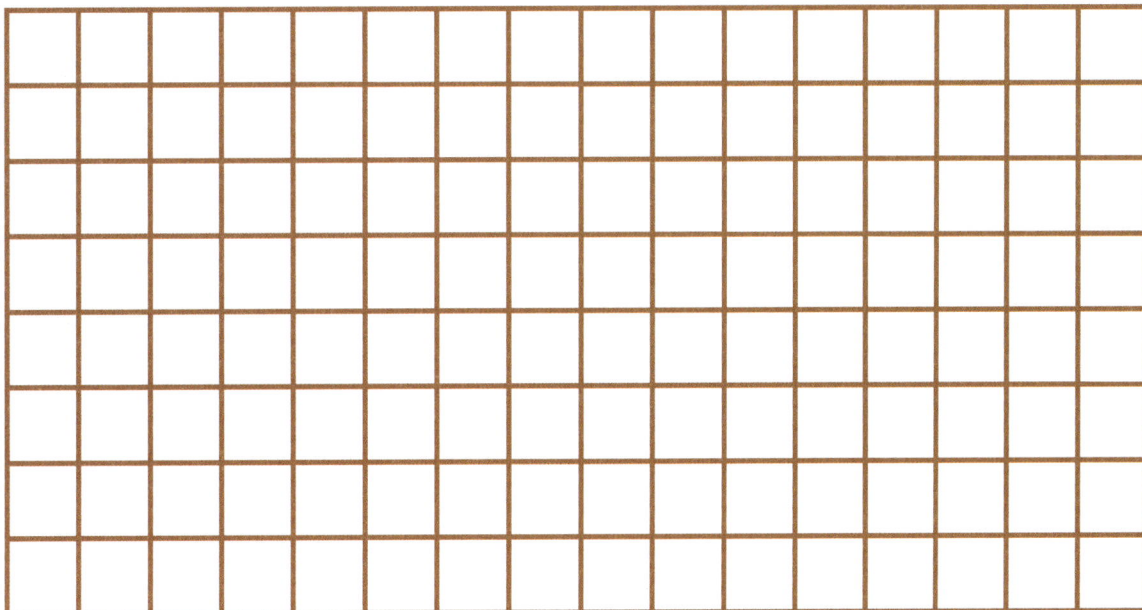

You need to know:

- How to describe in words the probability of an event happening
- How to calculate the probability of an event happening

EXAMPLE 1

Look at the probability scale below.

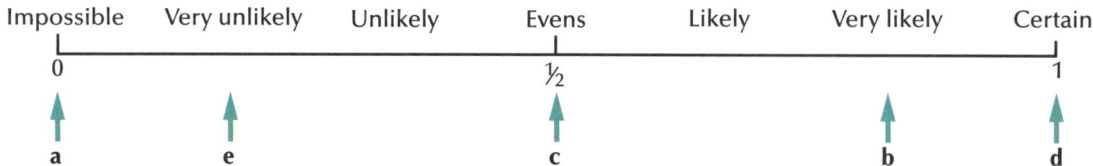

| Impossible | Very unlikely | Unlikely | Evens | Likely | Very likely | Certain |

0   ½   1

a   e   c   b   d

Draw arrows on the probability scale to show roughly the probability of the following events:

a You will live to be 180 years old – *Impossible*

b You will live to be 40 years old – *Very likely (but not certain)*

c A new born baby will be a boy – *Evens (could be boy or girl)*

d The day after Monday is Tuesday – *Certain*

e You will roll 6 when throwing a dice – *Very unlikely as there are 6 different numbers you could get*

> **Remember:** The probability scale goes from 0 to 1:
> 0 is impossible
> ½ is evens
> 1 is certain

> **Hint:** Always write probabilities as a fraction, decimal or percentage.
> **Do not** write as 1 out of 3, 1 in 3, or 1 : 3

EXAMPLE 2

What is the probability of each of the following events?

a Throwing a 5 with a dice?   How many 5s on a dice?   **Answer:** $\frac{1}{6}$
How many numbers on the dice?

b Drawing a King from a pack of cards?

How many Kings in a pack?   **Answer:** $\frac{4}{52} = \frac{1}{13}$
How many cards altogether in a pack?

> **Remember:** Cancel down fractions whenever you can.

> **Remember:** 30 days hath September, April, June and November. All the rest have 31 except February alone which has 28 days clear and 29 in each leap year.

Question 1

Underline the correct word to describe the probability of the following events happening:

a There are 30 days in January – *Impossible* or *Certain*?

b There are 29 days in February – *Very unlikely* or *Very likely*?

c There are 31 days in March – *Impossible* or *Certain*?

Question 2

A bag contains 2 red, 1 blue and 3 green balls. One ball is taken from the bag at random. What is the probability that it is:

a a red ball?   How many red balls in the bag? $\frac{\quad}{6} = \frac{\quad}{3}$
How many balls altogether in the bag?

b a green ball?   How many green balls in the bag? $\frac{\quad}{6} = \frac{\quad}{2}$
How many balls altogether in the bag?

c not a blue ball?   How many balls in the bag aren't blue? $\frac{\quad}{6}$
How many balls altogether in the bag?

> Underline the correct word in question 1, then complete question 2, remembering to cancel down in parts **a** and **b**.

1 Look at the probability scale below.

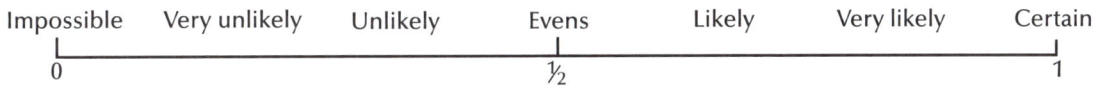

Impossible   Very unlikely   Unlikely   Evens   Likely   Very likely   Certain

0 ———————————————— ½ ———————————————— 1

Draw arrows on the probability scale to show roughly the probability of the following events.

a When you pick a card from a pack of 52, it will be a heart.

b It will snow somewhere in Great Britain next winter.

c If I throw a dice the score will be a 7.

d If I throw a coin I will get heads.

e If I exercise regularly and eat healthily, I will not put on weight.

f If I throw a dice the score will be 4 or less.

2 A bag of crisps contains 3 packets of cheese and onion, 2 salt and vinegar and 4 ready salted. Paul takes a packet from the bag at random. What is the probability that it is:

a cheese and onion? _____   **b** salt and vinegar? _____

c ready salted? _____   **d** not ready salted? _____

3 The numbers from 1 to 10 are each printed on a counter, and the 10 counters are put in a bag. Sian takes a counter from the bag at random. What is the probability that the number on it is:

a odd? _____   **b** a multiple of 3? _____   **c** prime? _____

4 In a school raffle, Susan buys 5 tickets. There are 650 tickets sold altogether.

What is the probability that Susan wins first prize? _____

5 A bag contains 5 balls. The balls are black, blue or green.

The probability of picking a black ball from the bag is $\frac{1}{5}$.

The probability of picking a blue ball from the bag is $\frac{2}{5}$.

Colour in the balls in the bag to show how many are black, blue and green.

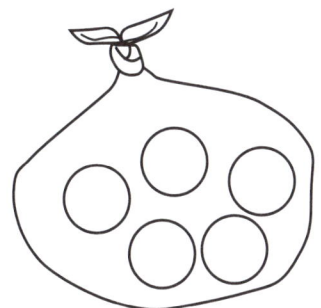

6 A box contains 12 tins of food with no labels. The tins are either beans, spaghetti, or custard.

The probability of picking a tin of custard from the box is $\frac{1}{6}$.

The probability of picking a tin of spaghetti from the box is $\frac{1}{4}$.

Label the tins in the box to show how many are beans (B), spaghetti (S), or custard (C).

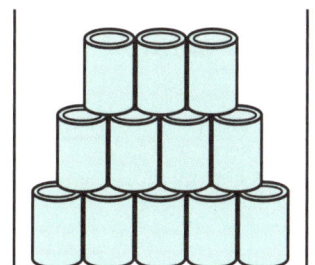

You need to know:

- How to work out the scale factor of an enlarged shape
- How to recognise congruent shapes

EXAMPLE 1

What is the scale factor used to enlarge shape A into shape B?

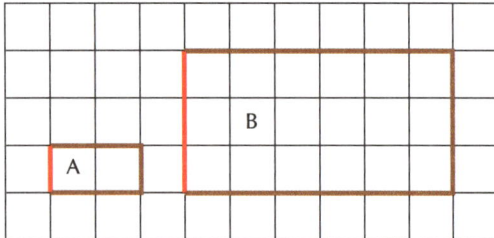

Compare one side of each rectangle – marked in red. Rectangle A is 1 square high and rectangle B is 3 squares high. $1 \times 3 = 3$, so scale factor is 3.
Check with other side: $2 \times 3 = 6$

Answer = 3

Remember: A scale factor of 3 makes all the sides 3 times longer than they were.

Question 1

Enlarge square C by a scale factor of 2.

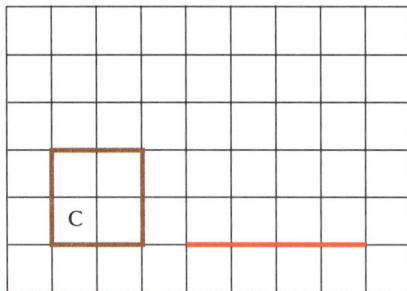

The square has a side length of 2 squares.
Scale factor is 2, so $2 \times 2 = 4$.
Length of sides of new square = 4

Complete the drawing of the new square in red.

EXAMPLE 2

Which of the triangles below are congruent to: ?

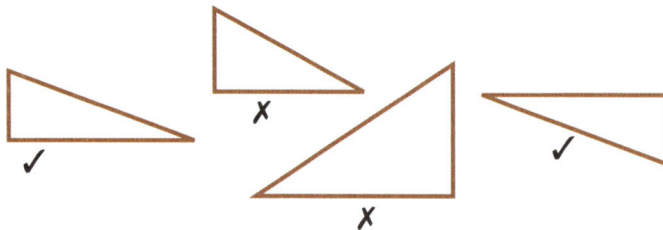

✓   ✗   ✗   ✓

Remember: Congruent shapes are identical; they are exactly the same size and shape.

Hint: Use tracing paper to trace the first triangle, then check whether it fits exactly on top of the others.

Question 2

Put a tick or a cross underneath the arrows below which are congruent to:

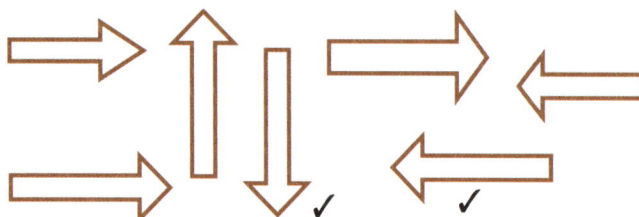

✓   ✓

Finish question 2. Use tracing paper to help if you want to.

1 What are the scale factors used to enlarge triangle A into triangle B?

a

b

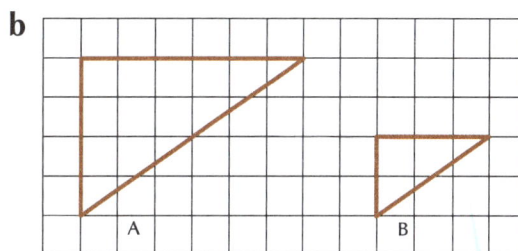

Scale factor = _____

Scale factor = _____

2 Enlarge shape C by a scale factor of 2.

Hint: In **b** triangle B is smaller than triangle A, so the scale factor must be a fraction.

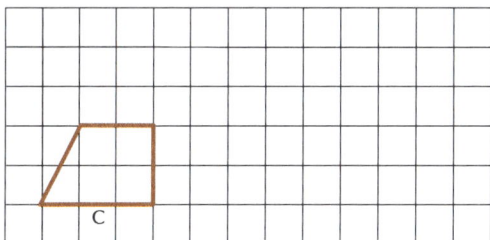

3 In the following sets of shapes, one is **not** congruent to the other three. Circle 'the odd one out'.

a

b

c

d

e

You need to know:

- Which units to use when measuring length, weight and capacity ● How to convert from one metric unit to and
- How to convert from one imperial unit to another ● How to convert from imperial units to metric units

---

EXAMPLE 1

Decide in which metric unit you would most likely measure each of the following.
a The length of a rugby pitch   **Answer:** metres
b The weight of an apple   **Answer:** grams

> To change **small** units to **larger** units, always **divide**
> To change **large** units to **smaller** units, always **multiply**

EXAMPLE 2

Do the conversions below.
a 25 mm into cm $25 \div 10$ **Answer:** 2.5 cm
b 4500 g into kg $4500 \div 1000$ **Answer:** 4.5 kg
c 0.55 km into m 0.55×1000 **Answer:** 550 m

Question 1

Work out the following conversions.
a 1300 ml = ? l   **Answer:** $1300 \div$ _____ = _____ l
b 2.55 t = ? kg   **Answer:** $2.55 \times$ _____ = _____ kg
c $3m^2$ = ? l   **Answer:** $3 \times$ _____ = _____ l

EXAMPLE 3

Do the following imperial conversions.
a 3 feet into inches 3×12 **Answer:** 36 inches
b 2 stone into pounds 2×14 **Answer:** 28 pounds
c 16 pints into gallons $16 \div 8$ **Answer:** 2 gallons

Question 2

Work out the following imperial conversions.
a 3 tons into pounds   **Answer:** $3 \times$ _____ = _____ pounds
b 4 gallons into pints   **Answer:** $4 \times$ _____ = _____ pints
c 33 feet into yards   **Answer:** $33 \div$ _____ = _____ yards

EXAMPLE 4

Use the conversion **1 gallon ≈ 4.5 litres** to convert:
a 3 gallons to litres 3×4.5 **Answer:** 13.5 litres
b 18 litres to gallons $18 \div 4.5$ **Answer:** 4 gallons

Question 3

Use the conversion **1 inch ≈ 2.5 cm** to convert:
a 8 inches into cm   **Answer:** $8 \times$ _____ = _____ cm
b 30 cm into inches   **Answer:** $30 \div$ _____ = _____ inches

---

Remember:
Units for
length are: km, m, cm, mm
weight are: tonnes (t), kg, g
capacity are: l, cl, ml

Remember:
length
  10 mm = 1cm
  100 cm = 1m
  1000 m = 1km
weight
  1000 g = 1 kg
  1000 kg = 1 t
capacity
  10 ml = 1 cl
  100 cl = 1 litre
  1000 ml = 1 litre
volume
  $1 ml = 1 cm^3$
  $1000 l = 1 m^3$

Complete question 1

Remember:
length
12 inches = 1 foot
3 feet = 1 yard
1760 yards = 1 mile
weight
16 ounces = 1 pound
14 pounds = 1 stone
2240 pounds = 1 ton
capacity
8 pints = 1 gallon

Complete
questions 2 and 3

Remember:
≈ means 'roughly equal to'

1 Decide in which metric unit you would most likely measure each of the following.

a The thickness of a £1 coin _____

b The amount of milk in a small cup _____

c The length of a swimming pool _____

d The weight of a rugby player _____

2 Work out the following metric conversions, then pick the correct answer from the three choices. Write the letter of the correct answer in the box at the end. The first one has been done for you.

a 4.5 l into ml	$4.5 \times 1000 =$	A 45 ml	B 450 ml	C 4500 ml	C
b 350 cm into m		A 0.35 m	B 3.5 m	C 35 m	
c 0.6 kg into g		A 60 g	B 600 g	C 6000 g	
d 5650 kg into t		A 5.65 t	B 56.5 t	C 0.565 t	
e 370 mm into cm		A 37 cm	B 3.7 cm	C 3700 cm	
f 25.5 km into m		A 255 m	B 2550 m	C 25500 m	

3 Using the conversion factors on the 'Help' page, work out the following conversions. Join with a line the question on the left to the answer on the right. The first one has been done for you.

Question	Working	Answer
a 32 ounces into pounds	$32 \div 16 = 2$	12 feet
b 3 gallons into pints		2 pounds
c 36 inches into feet		3520 yards
d 63 feet into yards		24 pints
e 4 yards into feet		80 pints
f 10 gallons into pints		42 pounds
g 2 miles into yards		3 feet
h 3 stone into pounds		21 yards

4 Use the conversion **5 miles ≈ 8 kilometres** to convert:

a 24 km to miles _____   b 25 miles to km _____

5 Use the conversion **2.2 pounds ≈ 1 kilogram** to convert:

a 6 kg to pounds _____   b 55 pounds to kg _____

1 Look at the probability scale below.

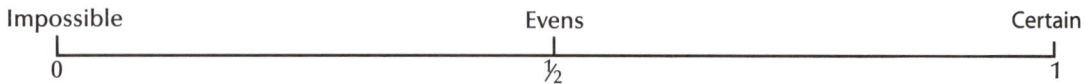

Impossible   Evens   Certain

0   ½   1

Draw arrows on the scale to show roughly the probability of the following events.

a If I breath in, eventually I will breath out.

b It will rain for at least one day next November in Bristol.

c If I choose a card from a pack of 52, it will be the 6 of hearts.

d If I flip a coin, it will be 'tails'.

2 A bag contains a set of pool balls. There are 7 red, 7 yellow, 1 black and 1 white.
If you choose a ball at random from the bag, what is the probability that it will be:

a white? _____   **b** red? _____   **c** green? _____

3 In another bag, there are 6 balls. The balls are red, yellow and black.

The probability of picking a red ball is $\frac{1}{6}$.

The probability of picking a yellow ball is $\frac{1}{3}$.

Label the balls in the bag to show how many of the balls
are red (R), yellow (Y) and black (B).

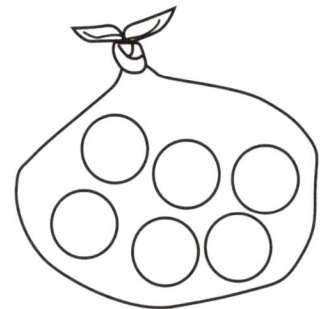

4 What scale factor has
been used to enlarge
triangle A into triangle B?

Scale factor: _____

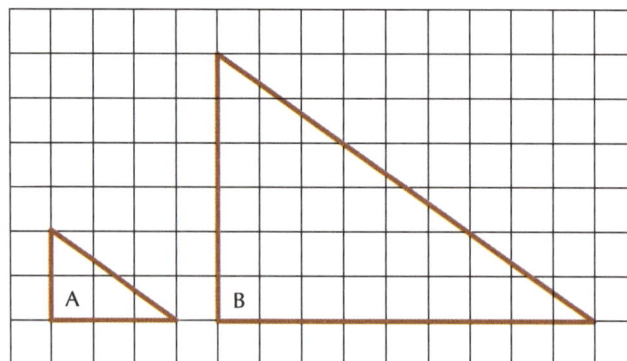

5 Enlarge this shape by
a scale factor of 2.

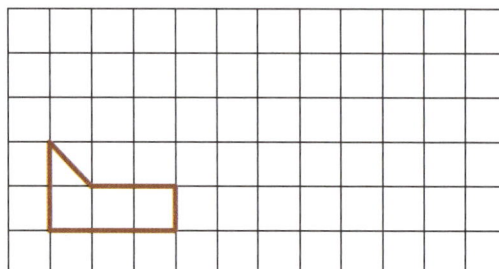

6 Are these shapes congruent?

Explain your answer _____

_____

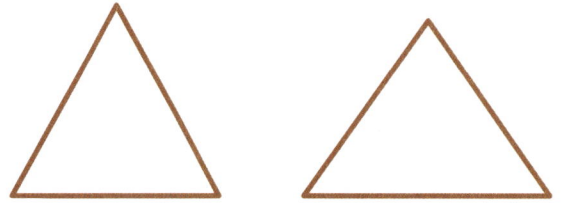

7 Which metric unit would you probably use to measure each of the following:

a The thickness of a pencil? _____

b The weight of a small mouse? _____

c The length of a motorway? _____

d The amount of water in a small pond? _____

8 Work out each of these metric conversions.

a 5 l = _____ ml

b 1.2 m = _____ cm

c 50 ml = _____ cm^3

d 1.2 km = _____ m

e 75 cl = _____ ml

f 0.1 kg = _____ g

9 Using the conversion of 5 miles ≈ 8 kilometres, convert the following:

a 48 km to miles _____

b 45 miles to km _____

10 Using the conversion 1 kg = 2.2 pounds (lb), convert the following:

a 9 kg to pounds _____

b 33 pounds to kg _____

11 **a** How many feet are in a yard? _____

b How many pounds are in a stone? _____

c How many inches are in a foot? _____

d How many pints are in a gallon? _____

You need to know:

● How to interpret pie charts ● How to draw simple pie charts

---

EXAMPLE 1

The pie chart shows the distribution of people at a cinema.

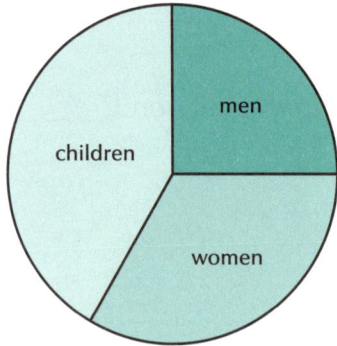

a What fraction of the people were men?

b Was the biggest group at the cinema men, women or children?

Measure the angles of the pie chart:
Men = 90° Women = 120° Children = 150°

a $\dfrac{90}{360} = \dfrac{90 \div 90}{360 \div 90} = \dfrac{1}{4}$

b Children were the biggest group

> **Remember:** There are 360° in a pie chart.

> **Hint:** When finding the fraction of a pie chart, always measure the section first, then make the fraction:
> $\dfrac{\text{degrees}}{360}$
> and then cancel the fraction down.

EXAMPLE 2

Use the pie chart on the right to show the following information:

Favourite sport of 10 children

Sport	Number of children
Rugby	3
Football	4
Cricket	2
Hockey	1

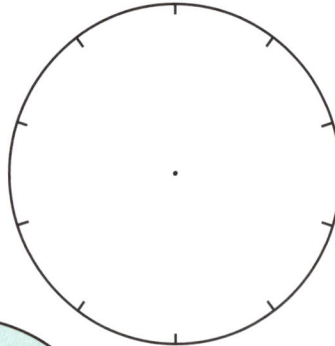

Answer:
The pie chart is divided into 10 sections, one for each child.

So Rugby needs 3 sections, Football 4 sections, Cricket 2 sections and Hockey 1 section.

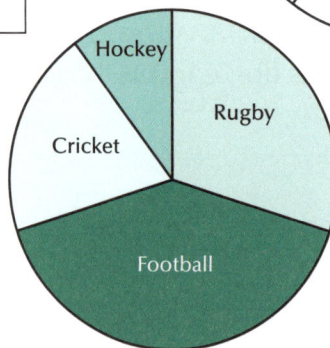

> **Remember:** Once the pie chart is drawn, label each section.

Question 1

Complete the pie chart on the right to show the following information:

The survey of a county showed that: 30% was built-up, 60% was farmland and 10% was rivers and lakes.

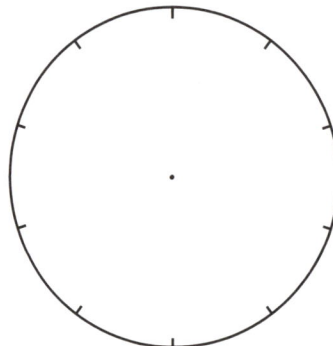

> Complete the pie chart.
> It is divided into 10 equal sections, so each section is worth 10%.

1 The following pie chart shows the results of a survey into what 100 people eat for breakfast.

a What was the least popular breakfast? _____

b What fraction of the adults ate cereal? _____

c How many of the adults ate cereal? _____

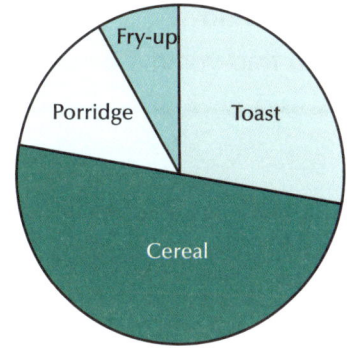

2 This pie chart shows the ways in which 800 students travel to college.

a Which two methods of travelling to college were equally popular?

_____

b What fraction of the students travelled by bus?

_____

c How many students travelled by bus?

_____

d How many students did not travel by bus?

_____

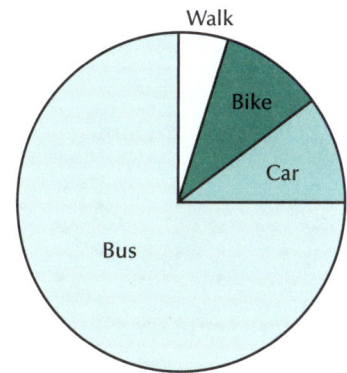

3 A survey was carried out on favourite holiday destinations in Europe. The results were:

Spain   40%

France   30%

Greece   20%

Other   10%

Complete the pie chart to show this information.

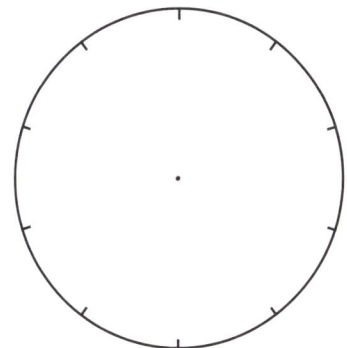

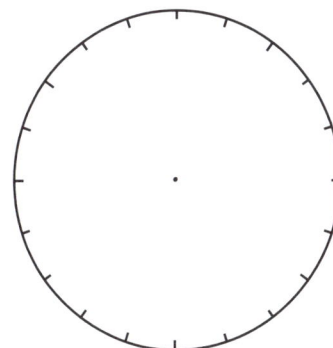

4 20 people were asked what their favourite 'take-away' is. The results were:

Indian   10

Chinese   6

Pizza   4

Complete the pie chart to show this information.

You need to know:

● How to find volume by counting cubes

> **Remember:**
> If each cube is 1 cm long, the units for volume are cm^3. If each cube is 1 mm long, the units for volume are mm^3.

EXAMPLE 1

Find the volume of each 3-D shape if the edge of each cube is 1cm.

a
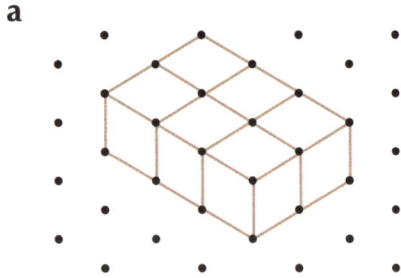

Answer: *6cm³*

b
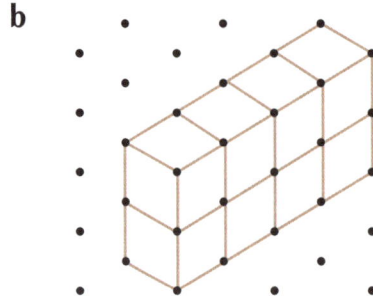

Answer: *8cm³*

> **Hint:** Try to count each layer, then add the layers, but don't forget the cubes you can't see.

c
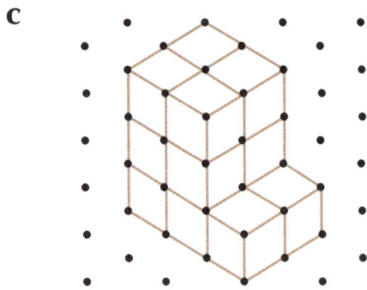

Answer: $4 + 4 + 6 = 14cm^3$

d
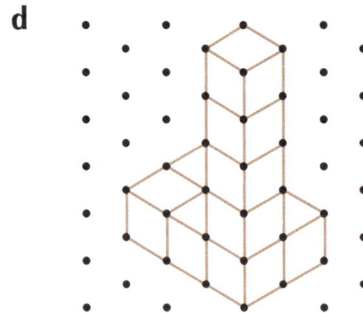

Answer: $6 + 4 = 10cm^3$

> **Example 1c:**
> top layer = 4
> middle layer = 4
> bottom layer = 6

> **Example 1d:**
> bottom layer = 6
> single column = 4

Question 1

Find the volume of each 3-D shape if the edge of each cube is 1 cm.

a
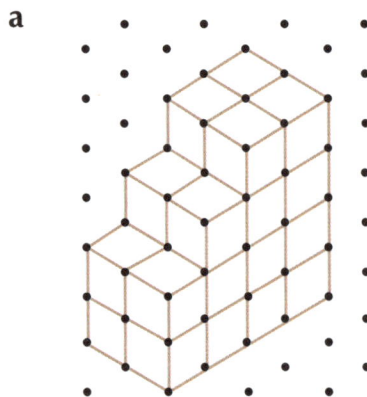

Answer: $4 + 6 + \underline{\quad} + \underline{\quad}$
$= \underline{\quad}cm^3$

b
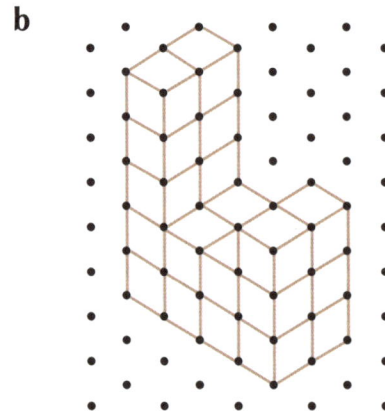

Answer: $2 + 2 + 2 + 2 + \underline{\quad}$
$+ \underline{\quad} = \underline{\quad} cm^3$

> Complete question 1.
> **a** top two layers already done.
> **b** top 3 layers already done.

Find the volume of each 3-D shape if the edge of each cube is 1 cm.

1
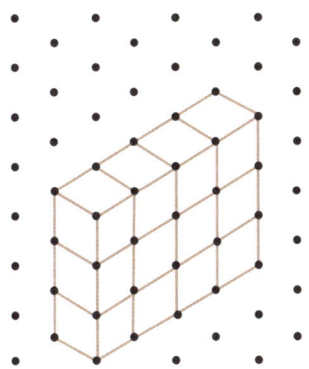

Volume = _____

2
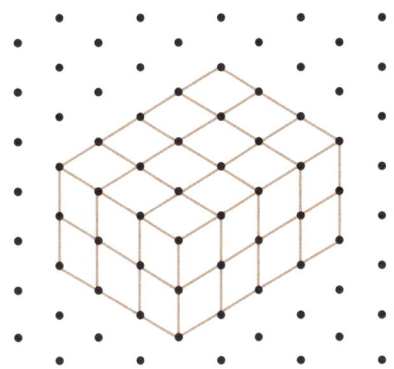

Volume = _____

3
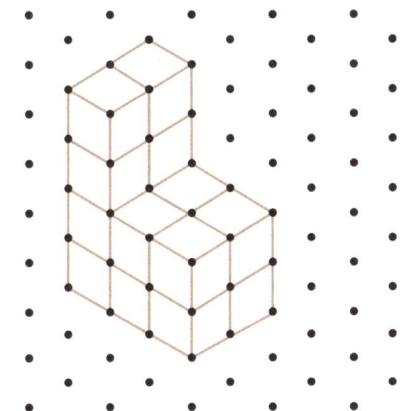

Volume = _____

4
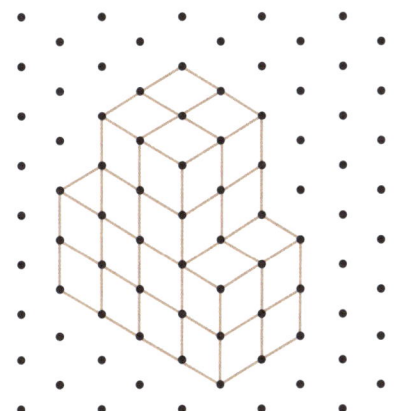

Volume = _____

5
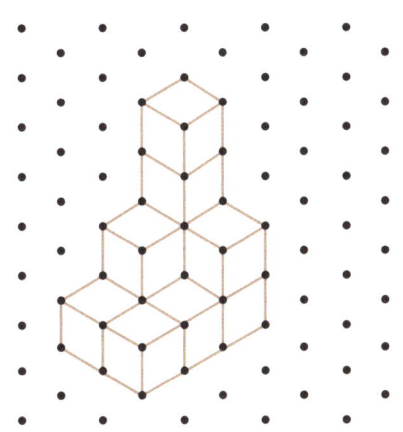

Volume = _____

6
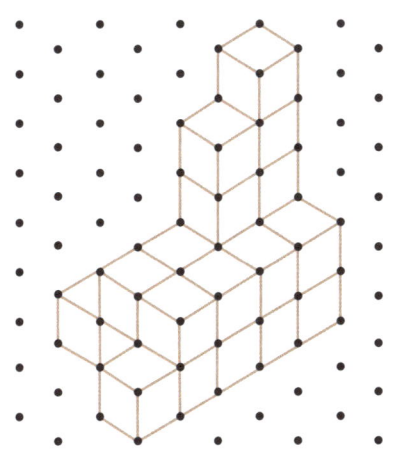

Volume = _____

1 This pie chart shows the results of a survey into what 1000 people drink for breakfast.

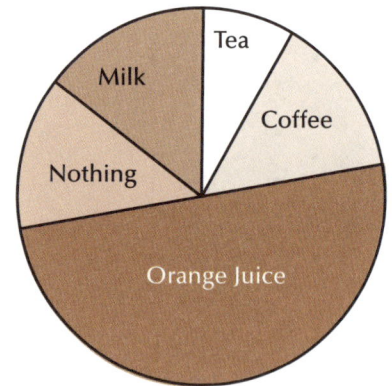

a What is the least popular drink shown?

_____

b What fraction of the people drink orange juice?

_____

c How many people drink orange juice?

_____

2 In Ali's school, the teachers gave out a questionnaire to all the students about what should be in the vending machines.
The results were:

A More healthy food and drink   60%

B More junk food and fizzy drinks   10%

C It's about right at the moment   20%

D Did not fill in a questionnaire   10%

Complete the pie chart to show this information.

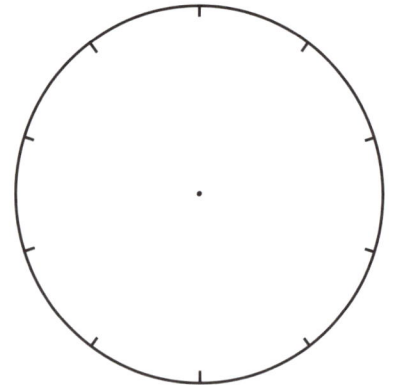

3 Twenty five students who did not complete the questionnaire in question 2 were asked 'why not?'
They said:

A Do not use vending machines   15

B Forgot to hand it in   5

C Couldn't be bothered   3

D Was ill and didn't get a questionnaire   2

Complete the pie chart to show this information.

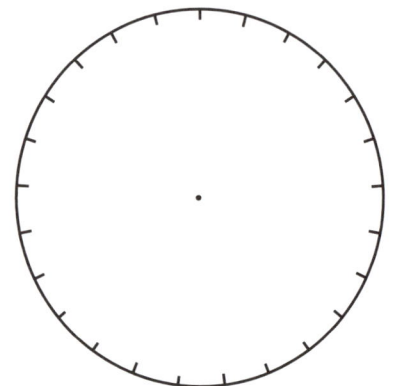

4 Find the volume of each of these shapes.
Each edge of each small cube is 1 cm long.

a

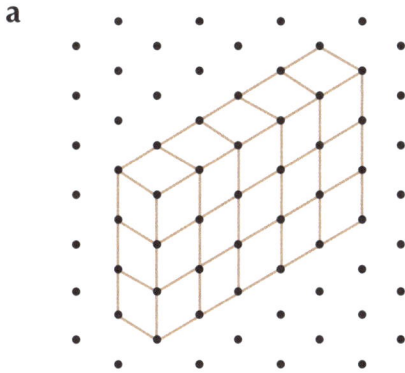

volume = _____ cm^3

b

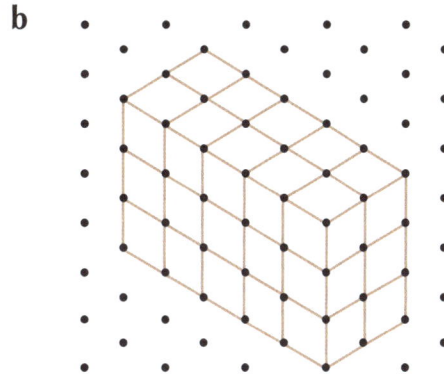

volume = _____ cm^3

c

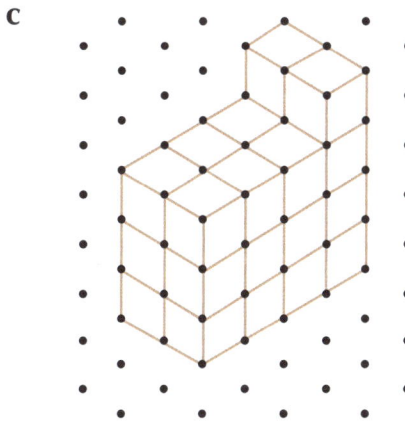

volume = _____ cm^3

d

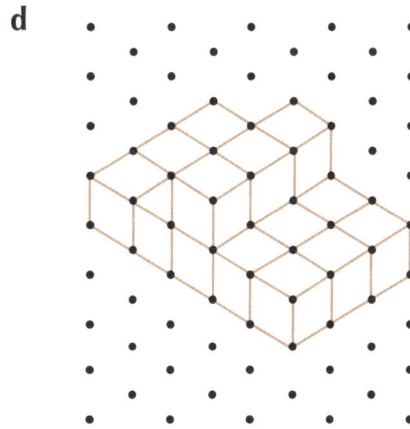

volume = _____ cm^3

e

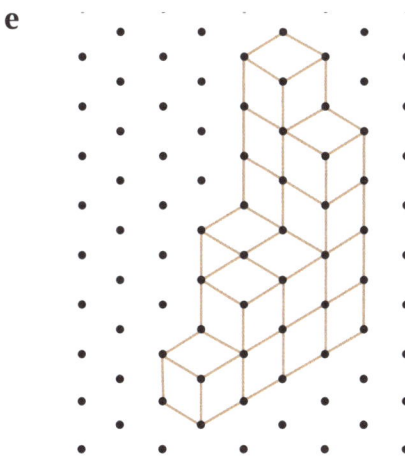

volume = _____ cm^3

f

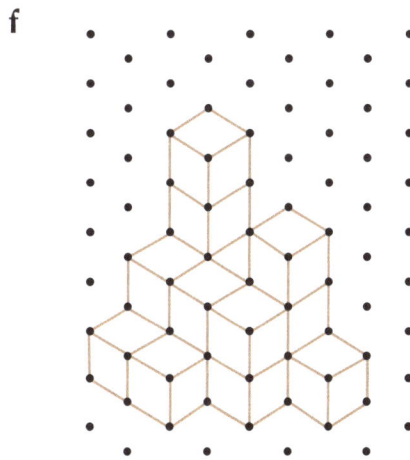

volume = _____ cm^3

95

Chapter 1 Addition

Question 1

a
```
  3  4  8
  4  6  8  +
  8  1  6
     1  1
```

b
```
1  3  4  8
5  4  6  8  +
6  8  1  6
      1  1
```

Question 2
```
4  1  7
2  0  5  +
6  2  2
```

Question 3
```
4  4  7  9
1  6  0  9  +
6  0  8  8
```

Question 4

a
```
2  6  .  7
1  8  .  4  +
4  5  .  1
   1  1
```

b
```
4  1  .  6  0
0  2  .  2  4  +
4  3  .  8  4
```

Chapter 1 Subtraction

Question 1

a
```
3  ⁶7̸ ¹0
1  3  7  -
2  3  3
```

b
```
⁴5̸ ¹3  ⁶7̸ ¹5
2  5  2  6  -
2  8  4  9
```

Question 2

a
```
8  5
4  3  -
4  2
```

b
```
⁷8̸ ¹⁰0̸ ¹1  9
2  9  6  0  -
5  1  5  9
```

Question 3

a
```
⁷8̸  .  ¹1
2  .  7  -
5  .  4
```

b
```
1  ⁷8̸  .  ¹2  5
0  4  .  5  0  -
1  3  .  7  5
```

Chapter 1 Multiplication

Question 1

a
```
1  2
   8  ×
9  6
```

b
```
      2  9
      4  2  ×
      5  8
      1
1  1  6  0
   3
1  2  1  8
   1
```

Question 2
```
      4  6
      7  ×
3  2  2
   4
```
$4.6 \times 7 = 32.2$

Chapter 1 Division

Question 1
```
    1 0 7
6 | 6 4 ⁴2
```

Question 2
```
    2 2 . 9
3 | 6 7 .¹8
```

Question 3
```
    0 7 5 9 6
7 | 5 ⁵3 ⁴1 ⁶7 ⁴2
```

Chapter 1 BODMAS

Question 1 $5 \times 10 - 1 = 50 - 1 = 49$

Question 2 $10 - 10 \div 5 = 10 - 2 = 8$

Question 3 $5 + 6 - 7 = 4$

Question 4 $3 \times (3 + 6) = 3 \times 9 = 27$

Question 5 $2 \times (6 - 2) = 2 \times 4 = 8$

Question 6 $(3 \times 2) + 10 = 6 + 10 = 16$

Question 7 $(5 + 15) \div 2 = 20 \div 2 = 10$

Question 8

Draw lines connecting the question on the left, to the working in the middle, to the answer on the right.

$4 + 3 \times 3$	=	$12 - 2$	=	18
$5 + (8 \div 4)$	=	9×2	=	10
$12 - 6 \div 3$	=	$13 - 4$	=	13
$(4 + 5) \times 2$	=	$4 + 9$	=	7
$8 + 5 - 4$	=	$5 + 2$	=	9

Chapter 1 Place value and rounding

Question 1

a two hundred or 200 b zero units or 0
c eight hundred thousand or 800000

Question 2 30   **Question 3** 2,100

Chapter 2 Fractions – shading and adding

Question 1 a Answer $= \frac{5}{8}$ b Answer $= \frac{3}{8}$

Question 2 Answer $=$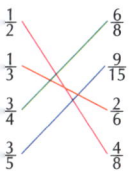

Question 3 a $\frac{7}{8} - \frac{2}{8} = \frac{5}{8}$ b $\frac{9}{10} - \frac{3}{10} = \frac{6}{10}$

c $\frac{4}{20} + \frac{7}{20} = \frac{11}{20}$ d $\frac{2}{9} + \frac{3}{9} = \frac{5}{9}$

Chapter 2 Fractions – equivalent and cancelling

Question 1

$\frac{1}{2}$ $\frac{6}{8}$

$\frac{1}{3}$ $\frac{9}{15}$

$\frac{3}{4}$ $\frac{2}{6}$

$\frac{3}{5}$ $\frac{4}{8}$

Question 2 $\frac{2}{3} = \frac{4}{6} = \frac{20}{30}$

Question 3 $\frac{40}{100} = \frac{4}{10} = \frac{2}{5}$

Question 4 $\frac{1}{2} = \frac{3}{6}$ $\frac{5}{6} = \frac{5}{6}$ $\frac{2}{3} = \frac{4}{6}$ Answer: biggest $= \frac{5}{6}$

Chapter 2 Fractions – topheavy and mixed numbers

Question 1 a Answer: **2** with 2 left over so, $\frac{16}{7} = 2\frac{2}{7}$

b Answer: **3** with 0 left over so, $\frac{18}{6} = $ **3**

Question 2 a $8 \times 3 = $ **24** $+ 2 = $ **26** Answer: $8\frac{2}{3} = \frac{26}{3}$

b $1 \times 8 = $ **8** $+ 3 = $ **11** Answer: $1\frac{3}{8} = \frac{11}{8}$

Chapter 2 Fractions – of an amount

Question 1 a Step 1: $240 \div 4 = $ **60** Step 2: $3 \times$ **60** $= 180$ Kg

b Step 1: $32 \div 8 = $ **4** Step 2: **7** $\times$ **4** $= $ **£28**

Question 2 a $400 \div$ **10** $= $ **40** g

b total weight $= 400$ g $+$ **40** g $= $ **440** g

Chapter 3 Negative numbers

Question 1 If +2 °C means 2 °C above freezing point, then **– 2 °C** means 2 °C below freezing point

Question 2 a **True**   b **False**

c **True**   d **False**

Question 3 a $5 > 3$ b $-4 < 3$ c $-5 < -4$ d $3 > 0$ e $0 > -5$

Question 4 a $6 - 7 = $ **-1** b $-2 - 2 = $ **-4** c $-20 - 20 = $ **-40**

d $-3 + -2 = -3 -2 = $ **-5** e $2 - -5 = 2 + 5 = 7$

Chapter 4 Multiples and Factors

Question 1 **10, 20, 30, 40**

Question 2 The multiples of 5 are 5, 10, 15, 20, **25, 30, 35, 40, 45, 50** Answer: **45**

Question 3 **1, 5, 25**

Question 4 **1, 2, 4, 5, 8, 10, 20, 40**

Question 5 **1** and **5**

Question 6 a 2 Answer: 1, 2   b 3 Answer: **1, 3**

c 5 Answer: **1, 5**   d 7 Answer: **1, 7**

Question 7 **2**

Chapter 4 Square, square root and powers

Question 1 1, 4, 9, **16, 25, 36, 49, 64, 81, 100**

Question 2 $20^2 = 20 \times$ **20** $= $ **400**

Question 3 **10** $\times$ **10** $= 100$ Answer: **10**

Question 4 **4** $\times$ **4** $= 16$ Answer: **4**

Question 5 a $10^4 = $ **10** $\times$ **10** $\times$ **10** $\times$ **10** $= $ **10 000**

Answer: **10 000**

b $2^6 = $ **2** $\times$ **2** $\times$ **2** $\times$ **2** $\times$ **2** $\times$ **2** $= $ **64** Answer: **64**

c $11^3 = $ **11** $\times$ **11** $\times$ **11** $= $ **1331** Answer: **1331**

Chapter 5 Shapes - area

Question 1 a Area $= 10 \times$ **2** $= $ **20** mm^2

b Area $= $ **length** $\times$ **width** $= $ **3** $\times$ **4** $= 12$ m^2

c Area $= $ **length** $\times$ **width** $= $ **27** $\times$ **1** $= $ **27** mm^2

Question 2 a Area $= $ **11** $+ \frac{1}{2} + \frac{1}{2} = $ **12** cm^2

b Area $= $ **8** $+ 0 = $ **8** cm^2

Chapter 5 Shapes - perimeter

Question 1 a $P = $ **4** $+ 2 +$ **4** $+ 2 = $ **12** cm

b $P = 80 + 20 +$ **80** $+$ **20** $= $ **200** mm

Question 2 a $6 - 5 = $ **1** m $4 - 1 = $ **3** m

$P = 6 + 1 +$ **1** $+$ **3** $+ 5 + 4 = $ **20** m

b **both missing lengths = 2 mm**;

$P = 2 + 2 + 2 + 6 + 2 + 2 + 2 + 2 = $ **20** mm

Chapter 6 Statistics – frequency tables and charts

Question 1 a

number of texts	tally	frequency
1	III	3
2	IIII	4
3	IIIII	6
4	III	3
5	II	2
6	III	3

b

Sun	🌕
Mon	🌕🌕
Tue	🌕
Wed	🌕🌕🌕
Thur	🌕
Fri	🌕🌕🌕
Sat	🌕🌕

c

Number of text messages in week 2

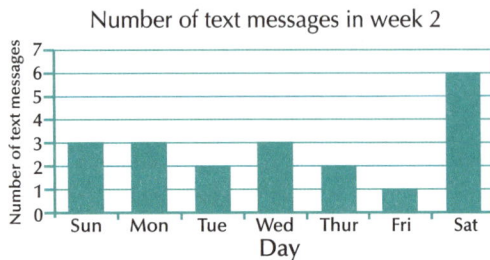

Chapter 6 Statistics – reading charts and sampling

Question 1 a January

b $3\frac{1}{2}$ mm

c November

Question 2 a 6

b 60

Chapter 7 Algebra – writing expressions

Question 1 a 5 less than a: $5 - a$ ⬭$a - 5$⬭ $-5 - a$

b b more than a: ⬭$a + b$⬭ $a - b$ ab

c c multiplied by itself: $c + c$ $2 \times c$ ⬭c^2⬭

d d divided by e: $\frac{e}{d}$ ⬭$\frac{d}{e}$⬭ $e \div d$

Question 2

Amy — y, $y + 2$

Brett — ~~$3y$~~, ~~$y - 2$~~, ~~$2y$~~, ~~$y + 3$~~

Carla — ~~$y + 1$~~, $y - 1$

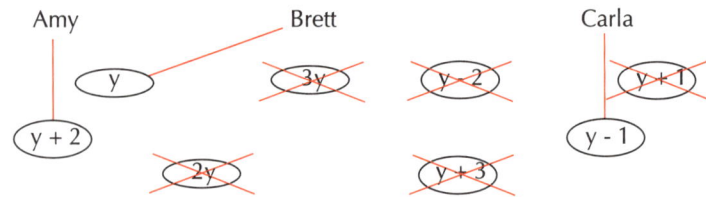

Chapter 7 Algebra – using formulae and sequences

Question 1   Cost = **12** × 8 + 20 = **96** + 20 = £**116**

Question 2   Cost = **1** × 15 + **3** × 10 = 15 + **30** = £**45**

Question 3 P = 4 × **10** = **40**cm

Question 4 a 16, 14, 12, 10, **8**, **6**   Rule: **- 2** each time

b 1, 3, 9, 27, **81**, **243**   Rule: × **3** each time

Chapter 8 Decimal rounding

Question 1 **6**

Question 2 **0.2**

Question 3 **9.38**

Question 4 **0.667**

Question 5 **£27.55**

Chapter 9 Ratio

Question 1 a 64 : 24 = 32 : 12 = **16** : **6** = **8** : **3**

b 2.5 : 3 = **25** : **30** = **5** : **6**

Question 2   3 hours : 1 day = 3 : **24** = **1** : **8**

Chapter 10 Symmetry

Question 1 a   b

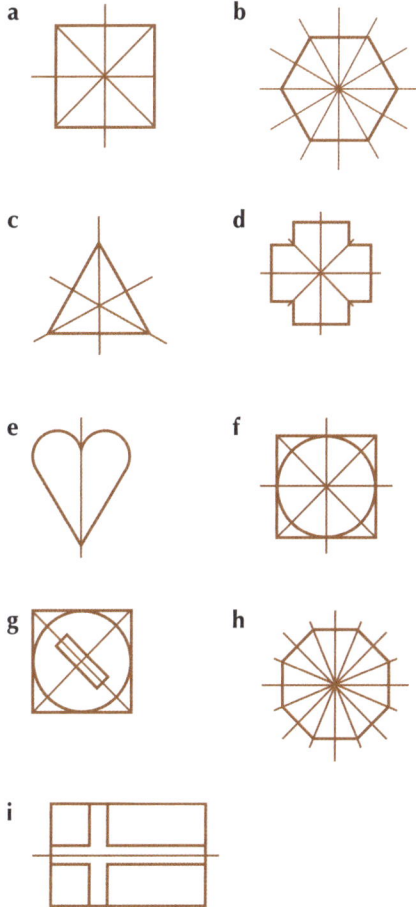

c   d

e   f

g   h

i

Question 2

Order 1	Order 2	Order 3	Order 4	Order 5	Order 6	Order 8
e i	g	c	a d f		b	h

Chapter 11 Averages – mean, median, mode, and range

Question 1

a   mode = **£3.15**

b   In order: £2.65, £2.85, **£2.90**, **£3.15**, **£3.15**; median = **£2.90**

c   Total of amounts = £3.15 + £2.90 + **£3.15** + **£2.85** + **£2.65** = **£14.70**
mean = **£14.70** ÷ 5 = **£2.94**

d   Highest − Lowest = **£3.15** - **£2.65** = **£0.50**
range = **£0.50** or **50p**

Chapter 12 Percentages, decimals and fractions

Question 1

a $25\% = \frac{25}{100} = \frac{25 \div 25}{100 \div 25} = \frac{1}{4}$

b $10\% = 10 \div 100 = 0.10$ or 0.1

c $0.6 = \frac{6}{10} = \frac{6 \div 2}{10 \div 2} = \frac{3}{5}$

d $\frac{3}{50} = \frac{3 \times 2}{50 \times 2} = \frac{6}{100} = 6\%$

e $0.056 \times 100 = 5.6\%$

f $\frac{3}{4} = \frac{3 \times 25}{4 \times 25} = \frac{75}{100} = 75\% = 0.75$

Chapter 12 Percentage of a quantity

Question 1

10% of £500	£45
10% of £7	£50
20% of £70	£54
30% of £150	£28
70% of £40	£14
90% of £60	£0.70

Question 2

home: 12% of 1600 = 12 ÷ **100** × 1600 = **192** pupils

sandwiches: 32% of 1600 = **32** ÷ **100** × 1600 = **512** pupils

dinners: 1600 - **192** - **512** = **896** pupils

Chapter 13 Algebra – solving equations

Question 1

INPUT	OUTPUT
3	3 × 5 = 15
5	5 × 5 = 25
9	9 × 5 = 45
35 ÷ 5 = 7	35
50 ÷ 5 = 10	50
100 ÷ 5 = 20	100

Question 2

a   x = 15 - 11 = 4

b   y = 9 + 5 = 14

c   w = 42 ÷ 7 = 6

d   z = 8 × 5 = 40

e   v = 18 − 12 = 6

f   y = 4 + 1 = 5

Chapter 14 Conversion graphs

Question 1 a **45**   b **15**   c **£33 approx.**   d **£17 approx.**
e **1.50**

Chapter 14 Plotting points and naming shapes

Question 1

2-D

triangle
square
rectangle
kite
rhombus
parallelogram
trapezium
pentagon
hexagon
octagon

3-D

cube
cuboid
square based pyramid
triangular based pyramid
triangular prism
cylinder
sphere

Question 2   **a** parallel   **b** neither   **c** perpendicular
d perpendicular   **e** parallel   **f** neither

Question 3   **a** A (1,1) B (5,1) C(7,3)   **b** D (3,3)

Chapter 15 Angles

Question 1   **a** 75° acute   **b** 195° reflex

Question 2   **a** d = **180**- 20 = **160°**   **b** e = 360 - **120** - **90** = **150°**

Chapter 16 Circles

Question 1   radius = $\frac{1}{2}$ of **5** = **2**$\frac{1}{2}$ cm

Question 2   **a**   **b**   **c**   **d**

radius   diameter   circumference   tangent

Chapter 17 Scale drawing and nets

Question 1   **800** m long

Question 2   **20** cm

Question 3

✓   ✗   ✓   ✗   ✗   ✓

Chapter 18 Probability

Question 1   **a**   Impossible
                 b   Very unlikely
                 c   Certain

Question 2   **a** $\frac{2}{6} = \frac{1}{3}$ **b** $\frac{3}{6} = \frac{1}{2}$ **c** $\frac{5}{6}$

Chapter 19 Transformations

Question 1

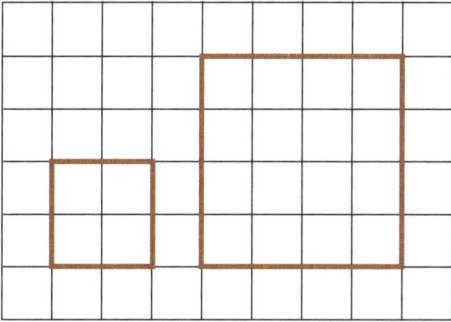

Question 2

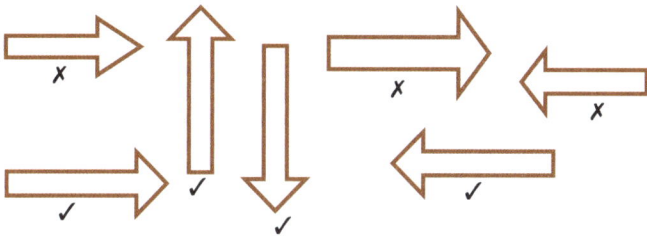

Chapter 21 Units

Question 1
  a 1300 ml = 1300 ÷ **1000** = **1.3** l

  b 2.55t = 2.55 × **1000** = **2550** Kg

  c 3 m^3 = 3 × **1000** = **3000** l

Question 2
  a 3 ton = 3 × **2240** = **6720** pounds

  b 4 gallons = 4 × **8** = **32** pints

  c 33 feet = 33 ÷ **3** = **11** yards

Question 3
  a 8 inches = 8 × **2.5** = **20** cm

  b 30 cm = 30 ÷ **2.5** = **12** inches

Chapter 22 Pie charts

Question 1

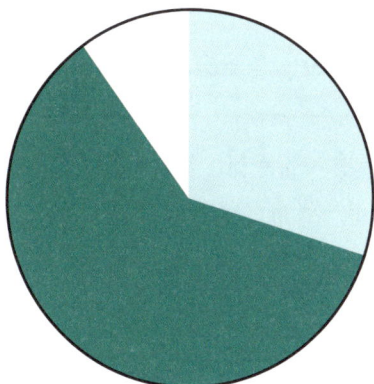

- built-up
- farmland
- rivers/lakes

Chapter 24 Volume of 3-D shapes

Question 1
  a 4 + 6 + **8** + **8** = **26** cm^3

  b 2 + 2 + 2 + 2 + **8** + **8** = **24** cm^3

g 8

Chapter 1 Addition

1   **a** 12   **b** 125   **c** 430   **d** 2188   **e** 1570
2   **a** $8 + 6 = 14$ **b** $24 + 87 = 111$ **c** $1284 + 436 = 1720$
3   **a** 36.1   **b** 22.02   **c** 219.522   **d** 26.3   **e** 30.06
4   £182
5   £22.74
6   921 people

Chapter 1 Subtraction

1   **a** 52   **b** 48   **c** 44   **d** 2928   **e** 58
2   **a** $28 - 12 = 16$ **b** $373 - 145 = 228$ **c** $5252 - 2525 = 2727$
3   **a** 2.7   **b** 4.8   **c** 1.75   **d** 22.4   **e** 4.73
4   £233
5   77cm
6   £184.65

Chapter 1 Multiplication

1   **a** 98   **b** 245   **c** 1687   **d** 820   **e** 824
2   **a** 378   **b** 1295   **c** 1107
3   **a** 3744   **b** 8995   **c** 15756
4   **a** 140.4   **b** 3.08   **c** 45.25
5   624 people

Chapter 1 Division

1   **a** 23   **b** 19   **c** 266   **d** 358
2   **a** 123   **b** 121   **c** 222   **d** 640
3   **a** 31.2   **b** 6.2   **c** 17.4
4   **a** 1.23   **b** 0.345
5   **a** 16.2   **b** 0.345
6   £546
7   15 miles
8   £56

Chapter 1 BODMAS

1   **a** 11   **b** 20   **c** 8   **d** 12   **e** 11   **f** 20   **g** 8   **h** 4   **i** 38
2   **a** 12   **b** 2   **c** 5   **d** 50   **e** 25   **f** 6   **g** 21   **h** 18   **i** 3
3   **a** +(iii)   **b** +(vi)   **c** +(i)   **d** +(v)   **e** +(ii)
    f +(iv)
4   **a** F   **b** F   **c** T   **d** T
5   **a** $4 \times (2 + 1) = 12$ **b** $2 \times (8 - 5) = 6$ **c** $(12 \div 3) + 3 = 7$
    d $(4 + 2) \times 4 = 24$ **e** $12 - (3 \times 3) = 3$ **f** $(3 + 3) \times 4 = 24$
6   **a** $(2 + 3) \times 4 = 20$ **b** $2 \times 3 - 4 = 2$ **c** $2 + 3 - 4 = 1$
    d $2 \times (3 + 4) = 14$

Chapter 1 Place value and rounding

1   Tens of thousands, Tens
2   **a** 6 units   **b** seventy thousand or 70000   **c** 0 hundreds
    d ninety or 90   **e** eight hundred thousand or 800 000
    f four thousand or 4000
3   **a** 99, 129, 201, 210, 378, 567, 800

    b 12, 112, 292, 303, 333, 292, 929, 2009
4   **a** 80   **b** 100   **c** 3100   **d** 3000   **e** 27 000   **f** 27 500
    g 1800   **h** 1000
5   **a** T   **b** F   **c** T   **d** F

Chapter 2 Fractions – shading and adding

1   **a** $\frac{3}{4}$ **b** $\frac{1}{6}$ **c** $\frac{8}{16} = \frac{1}{2}$
2   **a** 3 out of 4 shaded   **b** 1 out of 4 equal parts shaded
    c 2 out of 3 shaded   **d** 1 out of 6 equal parts shaded.
3   **a** $\frac{5}{7}$ **b** $\frac{4}{5}$ **c** $\frac{2}{8} = \frac{1}{4}$ **d** $\frac{4}{20} = \frac{1}{5}$
4   **a** +(iii)   **b** +(iv)   **c** +(i)   **d** +(ii)
5   **a** 4 equal sections, 2 of them shaded   **c** i $\frac{3}{4}$ ii $\frac{1}{4}$

Chapter 2 Fractions – equivalent and cancelling

1   **a** $\frac{1}{2} = \frac{2}{4} = \frac{3}{6} = \frac{4}{8} = \frac{5}{10} = \frac{10}{20}$ **b** $\frac{3}{5} = \frac{6}{10} = \frac{9}{15} = \frac{12}{20} = \frac{15}{25} = \frac{3}{5}$
2   $\frac{1}{2} = \frac{5}{10}$ $\frac{1}{4} = \frac{5}{20}$ $\frac{1}{3} = \frac{10}{30}$ $\frac{3}{10} = \frac{6}{20}$ $\frac{2}{5} = \frac{4}{10}$
3   **a** $\frac{3}{10}$ **b** $\frac{2}{3}$ **c** $\frac{4}{5}$ **d** $\frac{1}{4}$
4   **a** $\frac{1}{3}, \frac{1}{2}, \frac{4}{6}$ **b** $\frac{6}{10}, \frac{2}{3}, \frac{4}{5}$

Chapter 2 Fractions – top heavy and mixed numbers

a $1\frac{1}{2}$ **b** 2 **c** $2\frac{1}{2}$ **d** $2\frac{2}{3}$ **e** 3 **f** $3\frac{1}{3}$ **g** $2\frac{3}{5}$ **h** $2\frac{4}{5}$
i 3 **j** $9\frac{9}{10}$ **k** 10 **l** $10\frac{1}{10}$

a $\frac{5}{2}$ **b** $\frac{7}{2}$ **c** $\frac{9}{2}$ **d** $\frac{7}{3}$ **e** $\frac{11}{3}$ **f** $\frac{13}{3}$ **g** $\frac{26}{3}$ **h** $\frac{31}{4}$ **i** $\frac{34}{5}$
j $\frac{35}{6}$ **k** $\frac{34}{7}$ **l** $\frac{31}{8}$

a $5\frac{1}{2}$ **b** $5\frac{2}{3}$ **c** $\frac{23}{4}$ **d** $\frac{32}{3}$

Chapter 2 Fractions – of an amount

a 8 **b** 6 **c** 3 **d** 6 **e** 15 **f** 3

a 16 Kg **b** 18 g **c** £24 **d** 21m

a 100 g **b** 600 g

a £70 **b** £210

£3840

Chapter 3 Negative numbers

a -£100 **b** above

a -5 **b** 7 **c** any of the numbers from the list **d** -5 **e** 7
f -5 or -1

a -2 **b** -7 **c** 5 **d** -7 **e** -12 **f** -20 **g** 7 **h** -1
i -5 **j** -9

a 4 **b** 7 **c** 5 **d** -4

a +(iii) **b** +(iv) **c** +(i) **d** +(ii)

Chapter 4 Multiples and Factors

8, 16, 24, 32, 40, 48

24

multiples of 3: 6, 12, 15, 18, 24, 30, 33

multiples of 4: 8, 12, 16, 20, 24, 100

multiples of 5: 10, 15, 20, 30, 50, 100

multiples of 6: 6, 12, 18, 24, 30

a 1, 2, 3, 4, 6, 8, 12, 24 **b** 1, 2, 3, 4, 9, 12, 18, 36
c 1, 2, 3, 4, 12

a 1, 2, 4, 5, 7, 10, 14, 20, 28, 35, 70, 140
b 1, 2, 3, 4, 6, 8, 12, 16, 24, 32, 48, 96 **c** 1, 2, 4

5, 37, 13, 11, 111, 47

Chapter 4 Square, square root and powers

1 1, 4, 9, 16, 25, 36, 49, 64, 81, 100, 121, 144

2 **a** 49 **b** 100 **c** 64 **d** 9 **e** 4 **f** 6

3 **a** 900 **b** 8000 **c** 50625 **d** 100000 **e** 3125 **f** 1024
g 1 **h** 1296 **i** 35 **j** 45 **k** 55 **l** 65 **m** 75 **n** 85
o 95 **p** 25

4 odd numbers = 7, 9, 11, 15, 25, 49, 81

even numbers = 2, 12, 100

square numbers = 9, 25, 49, 81, 100

prime numbers = 2, 7, 11

Chapter 5 Shapes – area

1 **a** 20 cm^2 **b** 22 cm^2

2 **a** 15 cm^2 **b** 20 m^2 **c** 17 mm^2

3 31 to 37 cm^2

Chapter 5 Shapes – perimeter

1 **a** 18 cm **b** 28 cm

2 **a** 16 cm **b** 18 m **c** 36 mm

3 20 m

ANSWERS Practice pages

Chapter 6 Statistics – frequency tables and charts

1 a

Height in cm	Tally	Frequency
6	III	3
7	ⅢⅠ	5
8	ⅢⅠ	5
9	III	3
10	II	2
11	II	2

b

6	✳✳
7	✳✳✳
8	✳✳✳
9	✳✳
10	✳
11	✳

c

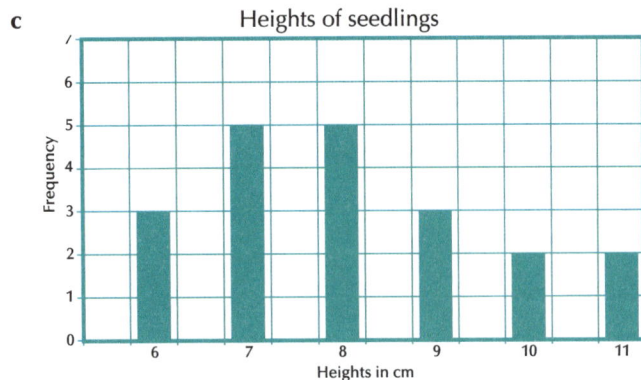

Heights of seedlings

Chapter 6 Statistics – reading charts and sampling

1 a Experiment b Take a sample c Observation

2 a July b 8 hours c October

3 a 9 b 34

Chapter 7 Algebra – writing expressions

1 a $x + 10$ b $x + y$ c $x - 10$ d $x - y$ e $\frac{10}{x}$ e $\frac{y}{x}$
g $10x$ h xy i x^2 j y^2

2 a $4a$ b a^2

3 Cleo = x Lomu = $x + 5$, Whoopee = $x - 2$

4 a $L = 4H$ b $A = 8O$ c $C = 3T$ d $S = 5P$ e $M = 10C$

Chapter 7 Algebra – using formulae and sequences

1 a 12 m b 18 m

2 a £50 b £90

3 a £50 b £85

4 a 12 cm b 27 m

5 a 16, 19, 22, +3 b 48, 96, 192, ×2 c 45, 55, 65, +10
d 12, 6, 0, -6 e 10, 5, $2\frac{1}{2}$, ÷2 f 40, 4, 0.4, ÷10

Chapter 8 Decimal rounding

1 a 43 b 52 c 2 d 4 e 12 f 15 g 3 h 81 i 99
j 67 k 13 l 9

2 a 5.2 b 6.8 c 8.9 d 14.5 e 11.6 f 58.5 g 8.6
h 3.8

3 a 4.66 b 3.34 c 8.88 d 11.32 e 32.90 f 14.32

4 6.2 5.5 8.49 6.24 7.91 8.6 5.51 6.4 7.9 8.882 7.90
5.488

Chapter 9 Ratio

1 a 2:1 b 3:1 c 3:1 d 2:1 e 5:1 f 4:1 g 4:1 h 4:
2 a 3:4 b 3:2 c 4:5 d 4:5 e 6:7 f 2:3 g 7:5 h 6:
3 a 1:6 b 1:4 c 5:1 d 7:1
4 a 3:10 b 1:3 c 1:8 d 7:3 e 1:20 f 1:4 g 1:8
h 6:1

Chapter 10 Symmetry

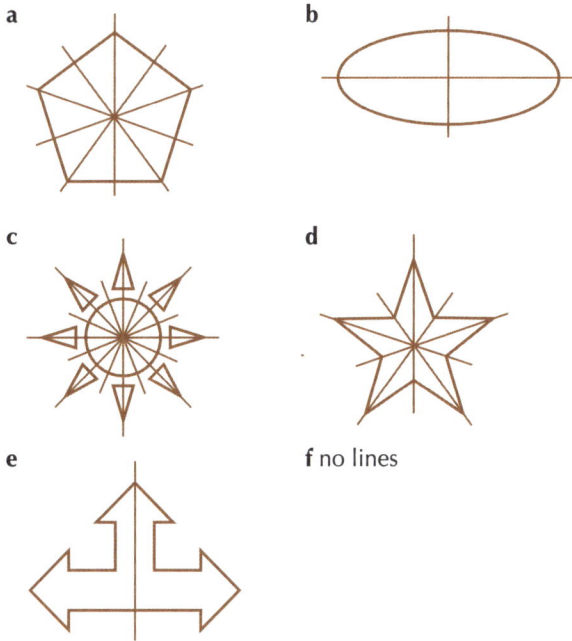

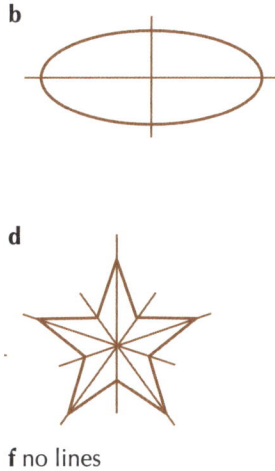

a

b

c

d

e

f no lines

a 2   **b** 2   **c** 4   **d** 5   **e** 1   **f** 3   **g** 1   **h** 2

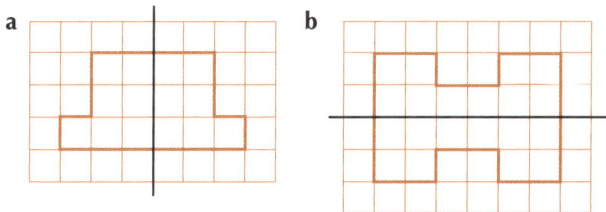

a

b

Chapter 11 Averages – mean, median, mode, and range

a 4   **b** 31   **c** 28 °C   **d** 6 °C

a 13 miles   **b** 12 miles   **c** 10 miles   **d** 10 miles

a 1 goal   **b** 2 goals

Chapter 12 Percentages, decimals and fractions

1

Percentage	Decimal	Fraction
25%	0.25	$\frac{1}{4}$
50%	0.5	$\frac{1}{2}$
75%	0.75	$\frac{3}{4}$
10%	0.1	$\frac{1}{10}$
40%	0.4	$\frac{2}{5}$
70%	0.7	$\frac{7}{10}$
20%	0.2	$\frac{1}{5}$
60%	0.6	$\frac{3}{5}$
45%	0.45	$\frac{9}{20}$
15%	0.15	$\frac{3}{20}$
17%	0.17	$\frac{17}{100}$
28%	0.28	$\frac{7}{25}$

2   35%

3   8%, $\frac{3}{10}$ (= 30%), 0.35 (= 35%), 0.63 (= 63%), 70%, $\frac{4}{5}$ (= 80%)

4   **a** 75%   **b** 60%   **c** 40%   **d** 55%

Chapter 12 Percentage of a quantity

1   **a** 7 kg   **b** £30   **c** 0.4 km or 400 m   **d** £0.80 or 80p

2   **a** $80   **b** 15 m   **c** £8.40   **d** 9 cm

3   £480

4   559 women

5   50 g

6   £1440

7   **a** £14.88   **b** £33.60   **c** £120.05

Chapter 13 Algebra – solving equations

1 **a**

INPUT	OUTPUT
10	2
12	4
14	6
20	12

b

INPUT	OUTPUT
9	3
12	4
21	7
36	12

c

INPUT	OUTPUT
4	29
14	39
24	49
81	106

2

Equation	Working	Answer
$x + 4 = 10$	$x = 10 - 4 = 6$	$x = 10$
$x - 6 = 13$	$x = 13 + 6 = 19$	$x = 50$
$6x = 60$	$x = 60 \div 6 = 10$	$x = 19$
$\frac{x}{3} = 4$	$x = 4 \times 3 = 12$	$x = 9$
$2x = 30$	$x = 30 \div 2 = 15$	$x = 6$
$x + 11 = 20$	$x = 20 - 11 = 9$	$x = 20$
$\frac{x}{5} = 4$	$x = 4 \times 5 = 20$	$x = 15$
$x - 25 = 25$	$x = 25 + 25 = 50$	$x = 12$

3 $y + 5 = 10$ ✓ $3y = 15$ ✓

$\frac{y}{2} = 10$ ✗ $y - 10 = 5$ ✗

$y + 12 = 18$ ✗ $y - 1 = 4$ ✓

Chapter 14 Conversion graphs

1 **a** $110 **b** $80 **c** £110 **d** £50

2 **a** £120 **b** £90 **c** $1\frac{1}{2}$ hours

Chapter 14 Plotting points and naming shapes

1 **a** square **b** pentagon **c** trapezium **d** triangle
e parallelogram

2 **a** cube **b** cylinder **c** square based pyramid **d** sphere
e triangular prism

3 octagon

4 arrow

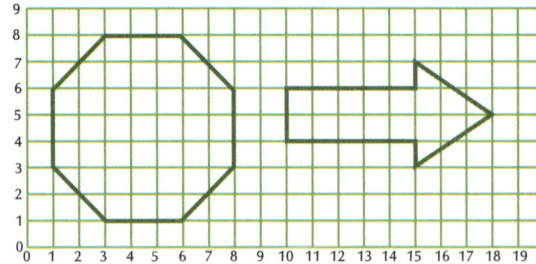

Chapter 15 Angles

1 **a** 40° acute **b** 150° obtuse

3 **a** 45° **b** 320° **c** 27° **d** 95° **e** 18° **f** 184°

Chapter 16 Circles

1 25 mm

2 7 cm

5 4.5 cm

6 84 mm

Chapter 17 Scale drawing and nets

1 **a** 16 m **b** 10 m **c** 3 m

2 **a** 12 km **b** 9 km

Chapter 18 Probability

1

Impossible	Very unlikely	Unlikely	Evens	Likely	Very likely	Ce
0			½			
c	a		d	f		e

2 **a** $\frac{3}{9} = \frac{1}{3}$ **b** $\frac{2}{9}$ **c** $\frac{4}{9}$ **d** $\frac{5}{9}$

3 **a** $\frac{5}{10} = \frac{1}{2}$ **b** $\frac{3}{10}$ **c** $\frac{4}{10} = \frac{2}{5}$

4 $\frac{5}{650} = \frac{1}{130}$

5 1 black, 2 blue, 2 green

6 2 custard, 3 spaghetti, 7 beans

Chapter 19 Transformations

a 4   **b** $\frac{1}{2}$

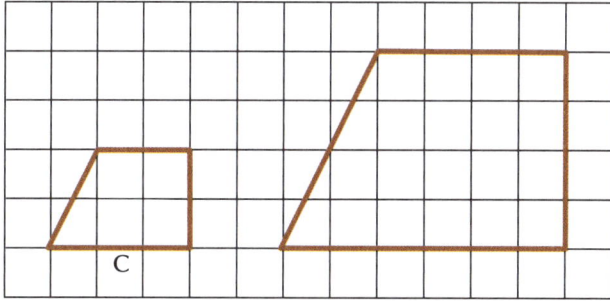

a 3rd **b** 1st **c** 4th **d** 3rd **e** 2nd

Chapter 21 Units

a mm   **b** ml   **c** m   **d** kg

a C   **b** B   **c** B   **d** A   **e** A   **f** C

a 2 pounds   **b** 24 pints   **c** 3 feet   **d** 21 yards   **e** 12 feet
f 80 pints   **g** 3520 yards   **h** 42 pounds

a 15 miles   **b** 40 km

a 13.2 pounds   **b** 25 kg

Chapter 22 Pie Charts

1   **a** Fry-up   **b** $\frac{1}{2}$ **c** 50 people

2   **a** Bike and Car   **b** $\frac{3}{4}$ **c** 600 students   **d** 200 students

3

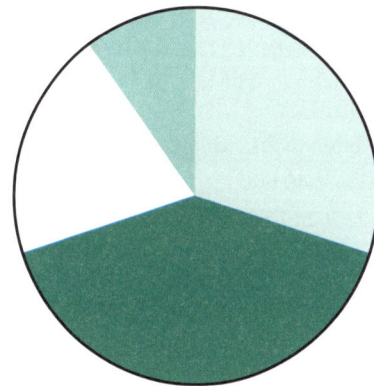

☐ Spain
■ France
☐ Greece
▨ Other

4

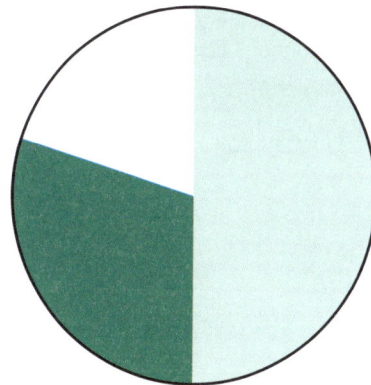

☐ Indian
■ Chinese
☐ Pizza

Chapter 24 Volume of 3-D shapes

1   12 cm^3

2   24 cm^3

3   16 cm^3

4   24 cm^3

5   11 cm^3

6   26 cm^3

Test 1

1   **a** 1174   **b** 47.22   **c** £36.74   **d** $\begin{array}{r} 2\ 7\ .\ 7\ 4 \\ 3\ 7\ .\ 1\ 2 \\ \hline 6\ 4\ .\ 8\ 6 \end{array}$ **e** 286

     f 27.58   **g** £217.50   **h** 372   **i** 2172   **j** 16652   **k** 14.48
     l £46.00   **m** 573   **n** 24.3   **o** £511   **p** 11   **q** 13   **r** 20
     s 5   **t** 9   **u** 2

2   **a** 2 tens or twenty   **b** ten thousand

3   **a** 49 500   **b** 49 500   **c** 49 000

4   £3.00 + £2.40 + £6.23 = £11.63

5   £10.00 - £6.80 = £3.20

6   315 g

Test 2

1   **a** $\frac{3}{8}$ **b** $\frac{10}{16} = \frac{5}{8}$ **c** $\frac{4}{8} = \frac{1}{2}$

2   **a** 1 out of 4 shaded   **b** 1 out of 4 equal parts shaded
     c 5 out of 6 shaded   **d** 2 out of 5 equal parts shaded

3   **a** $\frac{9}{12} = \frac{3}{4}$ **b** $\frac{10}{12} = \frac{5}{6}$ **c** $\frac{4}{12} = \frac{1}{3}$

4   **a** $\boxed{6}$ $\boxed{21}$ $\boxed{30}$ **b** $\boxed{4}$ $\boxed{50}$ $\boxed{16}$

5   **a** $\frac{1}{5}$ **b** $\frac{8}{15}$ **c** $\frac{3}{8}$

6 $\frac{4}{20}, \frac{1}{4}, \frac{3}{10}, \frac{2}{5}$

7   **a** $2\frac{1}{2}$ **b** 4   **c** $2\frac{2}{3}$ **d** $1\frac{3}{5}$

8   **a** $\frac{11}{5}$ **b** $\frac{32}{5}$ **c** $\frac{33}{10}$ **d** $\frac{521}{100}$

9   **a** 5   **b** 10   **c** 7

10   **a** 10   **b** 40   **c** 49

11   **a** £18   **b** 18 kg   **c** 12 m

12   **a** £100   **b** £200

13 $\frac{1}{3}$ of £240, by £8

Test 3

1   below

2   **a** -6   **b** 6   **c** -3, or 0 or 4 or 6   **d** -6 or -3   **e** 4 or 6

3   **a** -3   **b** -4   **c** 5   **d** -2   **e** -2   **f** -1

4   6, 12, 18, 24, 30

5   49

6   1, 2, 3, 6, 9, 18

7   1, 3, 9, 27

8   1, 3, 9

9   1, 2, 3 ,5, 6, 10, 15, 25, 30, 50, 75, 150

10   Any 10 of: 2, 3, 5, 7, 9, 11, 13, 17, 19, 23, 29, 31, 37,
     41, 43 ...

11   1, 4, 9, 16, 25, 36, 49, 64, 81, 100

12   **a** 16   **b** 36   **c** 10   **d** 8   **e** 8

13   **a** 289   **b** 4913   **c** 83521   **d** 59049   **e** 1000   **f** 28
     g 29   **h** 30

14   **a** 35 cm²   **b** 36cm²   **c** 24 cm²   **d** 18 – 22 cm²
     e 20 cm²

Test 4

1   **a** 24 cm   **b** 30 cm   **c** 20 cm   **d** 42 cm   **e** 28 m

2   **a** Observation   **b** Frequencies: 3, 5, 5, 3, 2, 2

     c

Height in cm	Key: ✳ = 2 seedlings
10	✳✳
11	✳✳✳
12	✳✳✳
13	✳✳
14	✳
15	✳

     d i 35   **ii** 30

3   **a** $x + 3$ **b** $y - 9$ **c** $\frac{y}{p}$ **d** p^2

4   Perimeter = 2a + 2b   Area = a x b

Test 5

1   18 cm

2   10€

3   **a** 21,25, add 4 each time   **b** 80, 160, double each time
     c 1, 0.1, divided by 10 each time

4   **a** 64   **b** 12   **c** 6.4   **d** 14.5   **e** 6.49   **f** 1.111   **g** 5.556

5   **a** 2 : 1   **b** 5 : 1   **c** 1 : 4   **d** 5 : 7   **e** 5 : 4   **f** 6 : 5
     g 3 : 4   **h** 1 : 5   **i** 12 : 1

6   **a** order 4

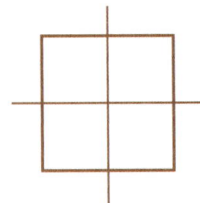

     b order 2

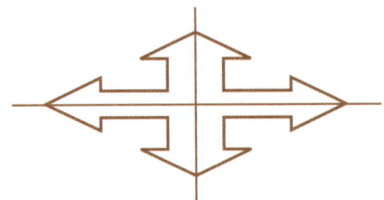

     c no lines, order 3

7

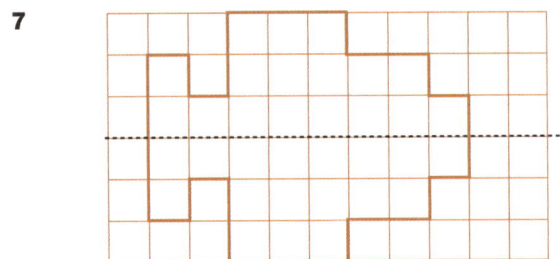

8   **a** 4   **b** 31   **c** 32°C   **d** 6°C

9   **a** 1.3 kg   **b** 1.2 kg   **c** 1.0 kg   **d** 1.0 kg

Test 6

Percentage	Decimal	Fraction
50%	0.5	$\frac{1}{2}$
75	0.75	$\frac{3}{4}$
30%	0.3	$\frac{3}{10}$
35%	0.35	$\frac{7}{20}$
5	0.05	$\frac{1}{20}$
65%	0.65	$\frac{13}{20}$

17% $\frac{2}{10}$ $\frac{1}{4}$ 0.26   99%

a 75%   **b** 52%

a 6 kg   **b** 50p   **c** 1.6 km   **d** 6 km

£78.75

output = 27, input = 43

a 6   **b** 13   **c** 5   **d** 3   **e** 27   **f** 200

a 90€   **b** £40

a rectangle   **b** octagon   **c** triangular based pyramid
d rhombus

0 triangular prism

Test 7

a 25°, acute   **b** 100°, obtuse   **c** 260°, reflex

a 60°   **b** 150°   **c** 290°   **d** 60°   **e** 140°   **f** 235°

a 2 cm   **b** 5 cm

5 m

a 14 m   **b** 3 m

a 5 km   **b** 6 km

Test 8

1
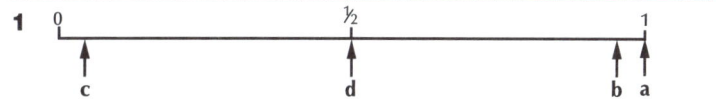

2   **a** $\frac{1}{16}$ **b** $\frac{7}{16}$ **c** $\frac{0}{16}$ or 0

3   1 red, 2 yellow, 3 black

4   3

5
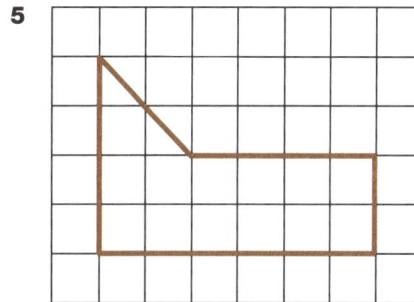

6   no, not identical

7   **a** mm   **b** g   **c** km   **d** litres

8   **a** 5000   **b** 120   **c** 50   **d** 1200   **e** 750   **f** 100

9   **a** 30 miles   **b** 72 km

10   **a** 19.8 pounds   **b** 15 kg

11   **a** 3   **b** 14   **c** 12   **d** 8

Test 9

1   **a** tea   **b** $\frac{1}{2}$ **c** 500

2
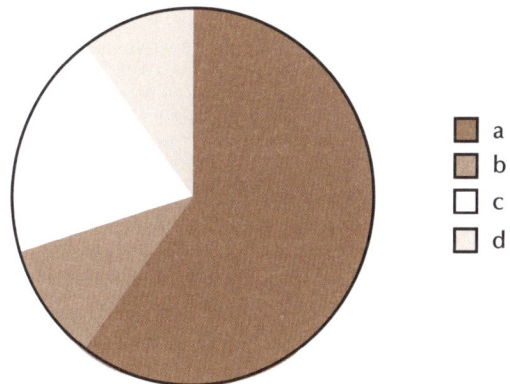

3
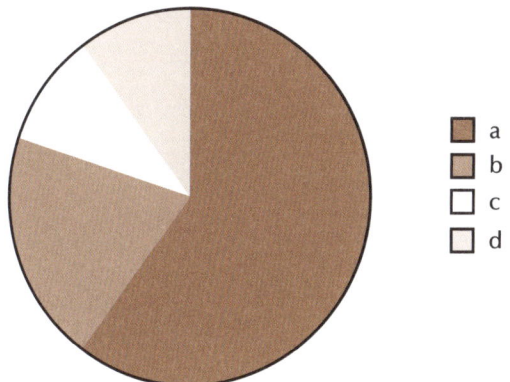

4   **a** 15 cm^3 **b** 30 cm^3 **c** 26 cm^3 **d** 18 cm^3 **e** 16 cm^3
f 18 cm^3

Workings

William Collins' dream of knowledge for all began with the publication of his first book in 1819. A self-educated mill worker, he not only enriched millions of lives, but also founded a flourishing publishing house. Today, staying true to this spirit, Collins books are packed with inspiration, innovation and a practical expertise. They place you at the centre of a world of possibility and give you exactly what you need to explore it.

Collins. Do more.

Published by Collins
An imprint of HarperCollins Publishers
77-85 Fulham Palace Road
Hammersmith
London
W6 8JB

Browse the complete Collins catalogue at
www.collinseducation.com

ISBN-13 978-0-00-721586-7

ISBN-10 0-00-721586-X

British Library Cataloguing in Publication Data. A Catalogue record for this publication is available from the British Library

Commissioned by Vicky Butt

Publishing Manager Michael Cotter

Project managed by Jennifer Carruth

Edited by Gwen Allingham

Cover design by Andy Parker and JPD

Internal design by JPD

Page make-up by Hart McLeod

Illustrations by Tim Oliver

Production by Natasha Buckland

Printed and bound by the Bath Press, Glasgow and Bath